THE COLLECTED POEMS
OF CHIKA SAGAWA

THE COLLECTED POEMS
OF CHIKA SAGAWA

Translated and with an introduction
by Sawako Nakayasu

MODERN LIBRARY

NEW YORK

The translation of this book was made possible by a generous grant
from the Japan Foundation.

JAPANFOUNDATION
国際交流基金

ISBN 978-0-593-23001-5
Ebook ISBN 978-0-593-23002-2

Printed in the United States of America on acid-free paper

modernlibrary.com

randomhousebooks.com

This translation is dedicated to Chika Sagawa.

CONTENTS

NEWLY COLLECTED POEMS

PROSE

INTRODUCTION

SAWAKO NAKAYASU

Sagawa Chika* is Japan's first female Modernist poet, whose work resonated deeply with, and helped shape, the most dynamic shifts and developments in the poetry of the era. I know this now after spending almost two decades with Chika's poetry, but at the time of my initial encounter in 2002, she was generally considered a "minor" poet—some even questioned my decision to translate her work in the first place.†

I first learned of Chika in John Solt's *Shredding the Tapestry of Meaning: The Poetry and Poetics of Kitasono Katue,* where he reflects upon his choice of PhD dissertation topic: "I could have focused on any of a dozen fine poets active before the war—such as Takiguchi Shūzō, Nishiwaki Junzaburō, Haruyama Yukio . . . and Sagawa Chika (1911–36)." I was intrigued to hear Solt mention a female name among this male-dominated group of poets, and my initial research indicated that Chika's work was long out of print, nearly impossible to access. The single exception was that a sixteen-year-old with the username "Ririka" had typed and posted all of Chika's poems on her blog. This is where I first read, and fell in love with, the extraordinary poems of Sagawa Chika.

Chika's poems are delightfully surreal. "Interrupted by thoughts,

---

* The book's title uses the Western convention, but here Japanese names are given surname first. In Japan there is also a tradition of referring to admired poets by their first name, in this case, Chika. A better-known example is the haiku poet Bashō, whose full name is Matsuo Bashō.

† Over my years of engaging with translation, literature, and education, I have come to feel there are elitist and careerist tendencies in the field that are toxic to the art. My thanks go to Keith Waldrop, who taught me and others to translate out of love, and to translate for art.

fish climb the cliff" is the final line of the poem "Afternoon," while in another poem, "The sky has countless scars. / Hanging like elbows" ("Like a Cloud"). Elsewhere, I found a sensual, emotional complexity: "Fingers stained with cigarette tar / Caress the writhing darkness. / And the people move forward" ("Backside"). I had never before read poetry quite like Chika's. I was still new at translating Japanese poetry, but I thrilled at the idea of sharing this work with other people.

To this day, I have only taken one formal workshop in literary translation, taught by the great poet and translator Keith Waldrop in the spring of 2002. Beginning to translate can be a fraught endeavor—there is a seeming abundance of potential errors, pitfalls, and failures. There is an assumption that one should be translating "the very best" texts in the most accurate, "faithful" rendering. Waldrop, brilliant iconoclast that he is, eschewed most conventional wisdom and encouraged us to translate what we most wanted to translate, and to "make it better in the translation"—he refused the conventional thinking that a translation was, by default, inferior to the original text. Thanks to his teachings—as well as my own youthful boldness—when I came across the poems of Sagawa Chika, the fact that she was a little-known poet, and that I was only beginning to translate, did not dissuade me.

It is now evident to more people that Sagawa Chika was a singular and deeply compelling poet, part of a global literary modernism.* Her influences include the Modernist Anglophone writers whose work she translated, as well as work from European literary and artistic movements, much of it translated or imported by her peers. Within this context, Chika's poems have a particularly idiosyncratic way of merging elements from her nature-filled upbringing with the cosmopolitan bustle of Tokyo. Despite her early death at the age of twenty-four, and her subsequent omission from the Japanese literary canon, her poems have leaped over time to reach

---

* See *Global Modernists on Modernism: An Anthology*, edited by Alys Moody and Stephen J. Ross, which includes Sagawa's prose piece "When Passing Between Trees."

a wider audience today. It is proof of the importance of her remarkable œuvre, created in less than six years of poetic production during one of the largest social and cultural shifts of her nation's history.

———

Sagawa Chika was born in 1911 as Kawasaki Chika (川崎愛),* to a family that owned apple orchards in Yoichi, Hokkaido, a small rural city with a population of about sixteen thousand. Nestled between the mountains and the sea in the far north of Japan, it is buried in deep snow for much of the winter. Frail from birth, Chika had difficulty walking until the age of four, and had problems with her vision. She had no father figure, but instead grew close to her halfbrother, Kawasaki Noboru. Against her family's wishes, she entered a girls' high school, and then went on to attain her license to teach English. In 1928 at age seventeen, she again disregarded her family's advice and moved to Tokyo, following her brother who had gone four years prior, as well as his friend Ito Sei, who had left for Tokyo four months before Chika and with whom she had a brief romantic relationship. By the time Chika arrived and moved in with her brother, the two young men had established some literary connections in Tokyo and helped usher her into their milieu.

Decades before Chika was born, the Meiji era (1868–1912) saw the overhaul of many fundamental aspects of Japanese government, economy, society, and culture. The old shogunate system was dismantled and eventually replaced with Japan's first constitution. Industrialization accelerated the rise of its military and paved the way for a horrifying, brutal history of imperialism that lasted until the end of World War II in 1945.† The Taishō era (1912–1926) saw the

———

* Her given name, "愛," was pronounced "Chika" or "Ai."
† Scholarship by Toshiko Ellis and William Gardner points to the activities of poets such as Anzai Fuyue (1898–1965) to show that contact with other Asian countries as a result of Japanese expansion had a specific relationship to the development of Japanese avant-garde poetics. See Toshiko Ellis, "The Topography of Dalian and the Cartography of Fantastic Asia in Anzai Fuyue's Poetry," *Comparative Literature Studies*, Vol. 41,

emergence of multiple and varied political parties and movements (including feminism and socialism), and was followed by the Shōwa period (1926–1989). The early Shōwa period preceding World War II was the moment of peak activity for the avant-garde poetry of Chika and her peers. They were not, for the most part, overtly political, but the fact remains that the boldness of their aesthetic experiments took place against the backdrop of Japan's intense nationalist ambitions, and these same engagements with foreign art movements would eventually become a liability, making them appear unpatriotic when such appearances were forbidden.

Meanwhile, in Tokyo, Japan's popular culture underwent great transformation. Restaurants served Western food, and jazz music played in dance halls and "jazz cafés." Young stylish people in Western-style clothing were, with either admiration or mockery, referred to as *moga* or *mobo*, short for "modern girl" and "modern boy"— they could be seen enjoying their "promenades" through the streets of the Ginza district. Chika, too, was photographed sometimes in kimono and sometimes in Western dress.

Modernism in art, architecture, and literature flourished during this early Shōwa period. In July 1923, just two months before the Great Kantō Earthquake, the radical art group MAVO was formed. Inspired by Dada and futurism from Europe, and in their explicit and sometimes violent rejection of the art establishment, they were the first to create a Japanese avant-garde. Many avant-garde poets likewise drew from similar influences and set about forming a new poetics. The fact that printing had recently become more accessible enabled art and literary groups to print and disseminate manifestos, pamphlets, and small coterie journals all over Tokyo.*

When the Great Kantō Earthquake hit in 1923,† the devastation it

---

No. 4, East-West Issue (2004), 482–500, and William Gardner, *Advertising Tower: Japanese Modernism and Modernity in the 1920s* (Harvard East Asian Monographs, 2006).

* Toshiko Ellis, "The Japanese Avant-Garde of the 1920s: The Poetic Struggle with the Dilemma of the Modern," *Poetics Today*, Vol. 20, No. 4 (Winter 1999).

† This earthquake destroyed over half of Tokyo, leaving more than 100,000 people either missing or dead.

caused had a profound impact on Japanese culture, and was followed by an intense period of reconstruction. Many saw this reconstruction as an opportunity for new cultural elements to take hold and alter the traditional ways of life.

> To fill the vacuum of the cultural past that had been swept away with the earthquake rubble, contemporary Western art, architecture, design, and literature were imported on a wide scale. Thus Dadaism, "destructive" of the tradition, spread easily in the atmosphere of constructing the new.*

Chika had a strong interest in paintings; other avant-garde poets were inspired by visual art, design, and film. They abandoned traditional poetic models like the *waka*,† made abundant use of foreign vocabulary, favored abstraction over narrative lyric, and absorbed the values of the Modernist texts they translated from French, English, and other languages. Japanese avant-garde poetry, though it had plenty in common with Western counterparts, developed within its own complex web of influences particular to the geopolitical and cultural shifts of the time.

—

In 1930, Chika met Kitasono Katue, one of the dominant figures in Japanese avant-garde poetry.‡ Upon reading her poetry, it was not Chika's adoption of foreign elements that impressed him—he simply recognized her tremendous talent as a poet, and instantly be-

---

* John Solt, *Shredding the Tapestry of Meaning: The Poetry and Poetics of Kitasono Katue (1902–1978)* (Harvard University Asia Center, 1999), 24.

† It was only a few decades earlier that *waka* was the only way for poetry to be written. In the Meiji era, Japanese poetry saw the development of a new branch of poetry that was radically different from *waka*, and the long-standing traditions of *tanka* and *haiku*. First was the arrival of *shintaishi*, which was later referred to as *jiyūshi* (free verse poetry). *Waka* continues to be written to this day, but ever since the Meiji era, Japanese poetry has been divided into these two main branches, with poets from one side rarely connecting with poets on the other.

‡ Miryam Sas, *Fault Lines: Cultural Memory and Japanese Surrealism* (Stanford University Press, 1999).

came one of the greatest champions of her work. He said, "The best poets often have their own complete identity from their first poem. Sagawa Chika was such a poet."* She was quickly immersed in Kitasono's literary community, joining the Arcueil Club, with the journal *Hakushi* (which later became *Madame Blanche*) as its publication outlet.† Chika soon became an influential member of the group, and even after *Madame Blanche* grew to encompass more than forty writers, she consistently stood out as one of the best. Kitasono described her as "naturally modest and quiet, but in the realm of poetry she wrote boldly and freely, like a princess . . . neither beauty nor death would pilfer nor even distort this freedom of hers."‡

Chika began publishing her poetry in 1930. The following year saw her first publications in the esteemed *Shi to Shiron* (Poetry and Poetics)—the publication hub for the avant-garde poets—beginning with her translations of James Joyce's poems from *Chamber Music*, shortly followed by her own poetry. Now Chika shared the pages with some of the most influential poets of the time, including Kitasono Katue, Nishiwaki Junzaburō, Kanbara Tai, Anzai Fuyue, and Haruyama Yukio. They published poetry, translations, essays, reviews, and *esquisses* (sketches), as well as special features on major foreign poets and ideologies. There was great aesthetic variation in *Shi to Shiron*, but the poets involved with the journal (and other smaller coteries with similar ideals) were grouped under the umbrella term *l'esprit nouveau.*§

* Sagawa Chika, *Sagawa Chika Zenshishū* (The Collected Poems of Sagawa Chika) (Shinkaisha, 1983), 224.

† The Arcueil Club, which later became the VOU Club, comprised many avant-garde poets of the day, including Nishiwaki Junzaburō. It was named after Arcueil, the Parisian suburb where the composer Erik Satie lived. Literary coteries were quite active at the time, printing self-produced journals that featured the works of their members.

‡ Kitasono Katue, *Kīroi Daen* (Yellow Oval): *Essays, Criticism, Scraps* (Hōbunkan, 1953). Quoted by Komatsu Eiko in *Ekoda Bungaku* (Seiunsha, 2006), 92.

§ The journal that Chika edited with Kitasono Katue was called *Esprit* and is referred to in several of her prose texts, like "Winter diary" and "Chamber music."

The *esprit nouveau* poets were in sync with the popular culture's warm embrace of French café culture, fashions, language, and literary culture. Thus it is likely that the pen name "Sagawa" (左川), written with the characters "left" and "river," alludes to the Left Bank of the Seine—the intellectual headquarters of Parisian artists and writers. In correspondence with the poet Uchida Tadashi, Chika wrote:

> Once we have some money, Ema Shoko and I want to set up shops in Ginza—she'll have a hat shop and a photography shop, I'd like to own a bookstore, like Sylvia Beach's.*

The Ginza district was home to Columbin, the first Japanese shop to emulate a French café. It was the fashionable place to be and be seen, as depicted in Chika's prose text "Ema Shoko and my radiant dreams." It is no surprise that Chika would know of Sylvia Beach, not only as the owner of the fabled Shakespeare and Company bookstore on Paris's Left Bank, but also as the first publisher of James Joyce's *Ulysses*, as Ito Sei was at that moment collaborating on the first-ever Japanese translation of the book.

———

Amid the frenetic activities of the literary community, Chika was also a bit skeptical of some of her peers, who seemed too keen to engage the trends of the moment. "When passing between trees" is a prose text that leisurely meanders through trees and wheat fields, eventually landing on specific commentary on poems by others.

> I wonder if the sun in May isn't a little too bright for the Japanese poets of today. They speak only of dreams and illusions, failing to harmonize with this all-too-French air. [...] They lose them-

---

* Chiba Sen'ichi, "Umi wa mitsuru koto nashi" (The ocean never waxes), *Sagawa Chika Zenshishū shiori* (The Collected Poems of Sagawa Chika, insert) (Shinkaisha, 1983).

selves only when imitating others, and when that figure has been chipped away at, are quite tired.

In comparison, Chika's poems wear their influence distinctly, but lightly. Her work is unique in its ability to straddle contrasting elements—East and West, nature and the urban, archaic and brand-new poetic lexicons. Her deftness at managing this dislocated, tenuous ground gives her work potency years after her death. While many Japanese artists struggled with their ambivalence about Western influence, Chika seems to have taken ownership of this tension. In the same text, she continues:

> It is not so much about searching for boundaries, but rather the precise snapping together of the infinite allusions on either side of that single line, with the cross-sections of a leaping field of vision. And yet, the highs and lows of artistic rhythm are determined by whether that field of vision is near or far.

While this statement resonates with André Breton's definition of surrealism as the juxtaposition of "two distant realities," it also enfolds the Cubist collapsing of foreground and background. Her relationship to visual art is further articulated in her prose text "Had they been the eyes of fish":

> I believe that the work of a painter is very similar to that of a poet. I know this because looking at paintings wears me out. Though I doubt there are many poems that are written with the same attention to the effect of color- or motif-based composition; the mood engendered by shadows; and lines determining their point of contact with space within a composition. I suspect that most poems are written with whatever random thought occurs to the poet. In some cases that's fine, although poems like that are already ruined. They are banal and have a short life span.

Fish eyes are more spherical than those of humans—with a greater refractive index, they are capable of bending light at a sharper angle. Furthermore, the fact that this refractive index changes throughout the lens provides for a sharp image with no optical aberrations, in spite of the spherical lens. In poetry, Chika's precisely broken lines allow us to read her poems not as fixed, stable objects, but as something more architecturally complex, inviting us to read, or see, the poem from multiple angles.

Modernism in Japanese poetry was more than just a break from the past. It was a difficult negotiation between old and new, one for which Sagawa Chika had special aptitude. Formally her poetry displays a radical break from traditional Japanese poetry (*waka*), and yet poems such as "Blue horse," "Spring," and "Seasons" use nature to depict seasonal change, very much in the spirit of *waka*. In contrast to the open exaltation of nature so typical of *waka*, though, Chika's depictions of nature tend to be threatening and ominous: "All shadows drop from the trees and gang up on me" ("Black air"). Chika's poems are neither conclusive, epiphanic, chronological, nor narrative. Instead, they originate in perception and emotional response, taking a form akin to collage and montage.

———

Institutional efforts to standardize the Japanese language had been initiated in the Meiji era and continued into the 1920s, but Chika and her fellow writers felt free to draw from foreign vocabulary, including words in Portuguese, Dutch, German, French, and English.* Likewise, creative use of orthography left room for the use of certain *kanji* (Chinese characters used in Japanese writing) that have since disappeared. Chika's poetry is exemplary of this multilingualism. Although the translations in this book do not emphasize these elements, some of her poem titles, such as "The mad house," "Finale," and "The street fair," were originally written in

---

* Here the term "borrowed" seems appropriate, as many words failed to find a permanent place in the Japanese lexicon.

English. Other poems use words written directly in English or via the phonetic *katakana* script used for foreign words.* Furthermore, even different versions of the same poem can illustrate how rapidly language use was evolving. For example, the "bread" in her poem called "Morning bread" was, upon first publication, written with the Chinese characters "麺麭," but was republished a year later with the same word written in *katakana* as *pan* (パン), taken from the Portuguese word *pão* and homonymous with the French *pain.*

Chika's work lived at the intersection of languages. Thus her literary translations also show her combining and remixing in this mode as well. Some of her poems are populated with Western personages that figure in the poems she translated—these include the Objectivist poet Charles Reznikoff's "Queen in May"† as well as the sailors in the poems of Harry Crosby. They also showcase Chika's unique ability to transform lines from the works she translated.

GATE OF SNOW

There are outdated beliefs piled up around that house.
—Already pale, like gravestones.
Cool in summer, warm in winter.
For a moment I thought flowers had bloomed
But it was just a flock of aging snow.

The last three lines are adapted from lines by Reznikoff: "The house is warm in winter, cool in summer"; "I thought for a moment, The bush in the backyard has blossomed"; "it was only some of

---

* For an alternative version of my translation of Sagawa that foregrounds the multilingual, see *Mouth: Eats Color—Sagawa Chika Translations, Anti-Translations, & Originals* (Rogue Factorial, 2011).
† This poem was collected in Reznikoff's book *Jerusalem the Golden* (1934). The fact that Chika published her translations in 1931 indicates that she most likely encountered it in an earlier journal publication.

the old leaves covered with snow." Her beautiful compression of Reznikoff's lines forges a middle ground between the writing and the translating of poetry. Chika transplants the lines of this Objectivist poet to a space that resonates more generally with her own tense relationship with the natural world.

A closer look at the activity of the Modernist poets opens up new relationships between translation, multilingualism, originality, and authorship. Moving one word of a text into a different language can be seen as a kind of microtranslation. The notion of a translator owning the words of a translated text upsets the assumed hierarchy that makes the original text primary, and the translated text secondary, and thus inferior. Ono Yū, an editor who scoured used bookstores in Japan assiduously collecting Chika's poems, in addition to beautifully publishing her collected poems, also published a collection of texts that Chika translated from English to Japanese. Here is a body of literature that might offer new insight into the relationship between translation and literature, beyond the current limits of our inherited practices.

———

In 1935, Chika was diagnosed with late-stage stomach cancer, and she succumbed to the disease in January 1936. Her last publications were excerpts of diary entries from her hospital stay, but even in earlier poems, the threat of death was never very far away.

Plans to publish a collection of her poetry did not come to fruition before her death. Ito Sei compiled and edited her work, publishing it with Shōshinsha that same year. Later, in 1983, Shinkaisha published a new edition that included poems discovered after the initial publication. The 2010 edition, upon which this translation is based, likewise added a few recently discovered texts.

Posthumous publication required that editorial decisions be made on Chika's behalf. Thus the poems are arranged in the order of initial publication, with the collection including all poems that have been published in any form. In a few instances, such as with "Beard of death" and "Illusory home," poems are so similar that one could argue that they are two versions of the same poem, but the editors have chosen to include both. The appendix of the 2010 edition includes extensive notes regarding variations on published versions of poems, through which one can see the differences in punctuation and style that might otherwise have been unified by the poet herself, had she been given the chance.

Chika's early death, along with the effects of World War II, prevented her work from finding a strong foothold in literary history. Even for writers who lived through the war, Modernist experimentation created a special set of difficulties. An FBI-like organization called the Tokubetsu Kōtō Keisatsu, also known as the Shisō Keisatsu or "Thought Police," had taken to arresting writers and intellectuals whose work was deemed unpatriotic. Poets were pressured by the government to prove their loyalty by writing patriotic verse. "Virtually every avant-garde poet cooperated with the war effort [...]. Almost any poet could serve equally well as an example, and a similar scenario of capitulation would have been observed."[*] Another prominent example is that of Nishiwaki Junzaburō, who abandoned his avant-garde pursuits in favor of the politically "safer" activity of researching classical Japanese literature.

While Japanese women poets have historically had a stronger presence in traditional poetic forms, there were very few who participated so rigorously in the intellectual explorations of the avant-garde. In that light, note the following words from Nishiwaki Junzaburō, upon Chika's death:

> Her poems were extremely honest, with a certain poetic heat at
> the core. There was absolutely nothing contrived in it; her poems

---

[*] Solt, *Shredding the Tapestry of Meaning*, 138. The chapter "The Quicksand of Fascism" gives a fascinating discussion of this issue via the work of Kitasono Katue. See also Samuel Perry, *Five Faces of Japanese Feminism: Crimson and Other Works*, for an example of a female proletariat writer who was arrested and jailed for antiwar activism, but also succumbed, eventually, to the pressures of the times.

felt truly alive. Even though she was a woman, I could see that her poems were enlivened by an intellectually clear and graceful thinking.*

Nishiwaki's mention of Chika's gender may seem patronizing to us today, but he made this statement in 1936. Rather, it is proof that their Modernist community was indeed male-dominated. *Shi to Shiron*, the nucleus of Modernist writing in Japan, published work by only a handful of women, and of them, Chika was the first and most prominent. Thus her work is notable for transcending this massive gender divide. Unfortunately, these are the same qualities that contributed to her obscurity, as her writing was not easily legible within established frameworks of "women's poetry," and later, of "Japanese poetry."†

Nationalistic tendencies continued in Japan as literary criticism picked up again after the war. This included the tendency to promote anything that appeared "authentically" Japanese, rather than that which seemed too heavily influenced by the West. Many of Chika's strongest champions were themselves pushed into oblivion by the cultural tides. Moreover, Western translators of Japanese poetry were attracted (through largely Orientalist inclinations) to work that read easily as "authentically Japanese."

Over the last few decades, Chika's poetry has steadily developed a contemporary audience. Reading her work in conjunction with that of other Modernists, beyond Japan and globally as well, high-

---

* Sagawa, *Sagawa Chika Zenshishū*, 239.
† By contrast, a poet like Yosano Akiko was innovative (and revolutionarily feminist) within the prescribed traditional form of the *tanka*. Her open, passionate poetic style directly addressed her feminine body, sexuality, and desires and made her poetry wildly popular among young women. She was extremely prolific over her long life and career, and had the strong support of her influential poet husband, Tekkan, who championed her work above his own. Toshiko Ellis discusses the importance of Yosano Akiko, Sagawa Chika, and Ito Hiromi in "Woman and the Body in Modern Japanese Poetry," *Lectora* 16 (2010): 93–105.

lights both the aspects of her work that are unmistakably Modernist and those that are entirely unique to her work. Chika has been an influence to many poets, most notably Yoshioka Minoru, one of Japan's greatest postwar poets. Her book is said to be one of the few that Yoshioka took with him while he was stationed in Manchuria during the war. The connections are visible—the prismatic architecture evidenced in Chika's poems foreshadows the layered montage in the poems of Yoshioka.

———

In addition to contributing to a wider conversation about global modernisms, Sagawa Chika's work makes a unique contribution to present-day considerations of multilingualism and translation in poetry. Chika has unfairly been cast as a "minor Modernist" or, a bit more lovingly, "everybody's favorite unknown poet." Fortunately, these labels are fading quickly, as more people have come to read, know, admire, and translate Sagawa Chika's honest, experimental, and sensually rich poetry. As Chika wrote in her poem "Smoke Signals": "And as life is burned / The time has come to spring into action." First, the action of reading this book.

Updated March 2020
Providence, Rhode Island

———

SAWAKO NAKAYASU writes and translates poetry and performances. Her forthcoming books include *Some Girls Walk into the Country They Are From* (Wave Books), *Pink Waves* (Omnidawn), and an anthology of twentieth-century Japanese poetry, coedited with Eric Selland (New Directions). Other books include *The Ants* (Les Figues, 2014), *Texture Notes* (Letter Machine Editions, 2010), *Hurry Home Honey* (Burning Deck, 2009), a translation of the butoh dancer Hijikata Tatsumi's *Costume en Face* (Ugly Duckling Presse, 2015), and *Mouth: Eats Color—Sagawa Chika Translations, Anti-Translations, & Originals* (Rogue Factorial, 2011), which is a multilingual work of original and translated poetry. She is currently working on a digital scholarly publication provisionally titled *The Past and Future of Chika Sagawa, Modernist Poet,* which considers the poetry of Chika Sagawa across a range of disciplines, temporalities, and media. She is Assistant Professor of Literary Arts at Brown University.

POEMS

INSECTS

Insects multiplied with the speed of an electric current.
Lapped up the boils on the earth's crust.

Turning over its exquisite costume, the urban night slept like a
    woman.

Now I hang my shell out to dry.
My scaly skin is cold like metal.

No one knows this secret half-covering my face.

The night makes the bruised woman, freely twirling her stolen
    expression, ecstatic.

MORNING BREAD

In the morning I see several friends escaping from the window.

Temptation of the green insect. In the orchard a woman stripped
of her socks is murdered. Morning, sporting a top hat, tags
along from behind the orchard. Carrying a newspaper printed
in green.

I, too, must finally go down the hill.
The city cafés are beautiful glass spheres, and a troop of men have
drowned in wheat-colored liquid.
Their clothing spreads in the liquid.

Madam with the monocle tears off her last piece of bread and
hurls it at them.

MY PICTURE

The villagers were surprised because the phone rang suddenly.
So does this mean that we must relocate.
The village mayor removed his blue jacket in a panic.
Yes, mother's allowance chart was indeed correct.
So long, blue village! The summer chased after them once again,
   like a river.

The rooster with the red chapeau disembarked at a deserted
   station.

RUSTY KNIFE

Pale blue dusk scales the window.
A lamp dangles from the sky like the neck of a woman.
Murky dark air permeates the room—spreads out a single blanket.
The books, ink, and rusty knife seem to be gradually stealing the
    life out of me.

While everything sneered,
Night was already in my hands.

BLACK AIR

In the distance, dusk cuts the tongue of the sun.
Underwater, the cities of the sky quit their laughing.
All shadows drop from the trees and gang up on me. Forests and
    windows go pale, like a woman. Night has spread completely.
    The omnibus takes a flame aboard and traverses the park.

At that point my emotions dance about the city
Until they have driven out the grief.

IT IS SNOWING

Upstairs from us, a grand ball!

Devious angels dance in disorder, and out of their steps fall shards
   of deathly white snow.

Death is among the holly leaves. Crawling quietly in the attic.
   Gnawing at my finger. Anxiously. And then at midnight—it
   falls at the storefront of the glass shop, exposing its stark white
   back.

Old love and time are buried, and the earth devours them.

GREEN FLAMES

I first see them loudly approaching descending numerous green stairs pass by look away cram into a small space while gradually hardening into a mound their movement makes waves of light furrow through the wheat field a thick overflowing fluid makes it impossible to stir the woodlands larch with short hair snail that paints carefully a spider spins electric wires like a mist everything rotates from green to deeper green they are inside the milk bottle on the kitchen table are reflected crouching with their faces flattened sliding around an apple they seem to crumble as they block off shafts of light in the street a blind girl plays by ducking under the shadows of the sun's rings.

I hurry to shut the window danger has come right up to me a fire blazes outside the beautifully burning green flames spread high, circling the outskirts of the earth and in the end they dwindle, disappear as a single thin line of the horizon

My weight takes leave of me takes me back to the depths of oblivion people are crazy here there is no point in feeling sorrow nor in speaking their eyes are dyed green believing grows uncertain and looking enrages me

Who blindfolds me from behind? Shove me into sleep.

DEPARTURE

Night's mouth opens, forests and clock towers are spit out.
The sun stands up and runs down the street of blue glass.
The city is cut into slivers of music by cars and skirts,
Then dive into the display window.
The fruit stand smells of morning.
Even there the sun multiplies in blue.

People throw rings at the sky.
In order to capture the suns.

BLUE HORSE

A horse came tearing down the mountain and went mad. From
 that day on she eats blue food. Summer dyes the women's eyes
 and sleeves blue, then whirls merrily in the town square.
The customers on the terrace smoke so many cigarettes that the
 tinny sky scribbles rings like the ladies' hair. I am thinking of
 throwing away my sad memories like a handkerchief. If only I
 could forget the love and regret and the patent leather shoes!
I was spared from having to jump from the second floor.
The sea rises to heaven.

VISIBILITY THROUGH GREEN

Visibility through a single acacia leaf
May   angels who discard their clothes there   legs dirtied
    green   faint smiles that chase me   memories glimmer before
    her as the neck of a swan

Now   where has the truth gone
Bird music congealed by evening mist   pictures of trees printed
    on the walls of the sky   a green wind gently flicks them
    off   Pleasure is on the other side of death   calling from the
    other side of the earth   Like watching the sun, grown heavy,
    dropping towards the blue sky

Run!   My heart
To her side   as a sphere
And then in a teacup

—Layers of love   they make us miserable   the furrows of milk
    waver   and my dreams rise up

BEARD OF DEATH

A chef clutches the blue sky. Four fingerprints are left,
—Gradually a chicken bleeds. Even here the sun is crushed.
Blue-suited wardens of the sky who come inquiring.
I hear daylight run by.
In prison they keep watch over a dream longer than life.
Trying to reach the outside world that is like the back of an
    embroidery, I become a moth that slams into the window.
If for a single day the long tendril of death would loosen its hold,
    this miracle would make us jump with joy.

Death strips my shell.

SEASONAL MONOCLE

Yellow-ripe and sick, autumn is the Arabian script staggering on
   the window.
All time goes to and fro here,
Transporting their vanity and music.
Clouds are burning such things as rooster thoughts and amaranth.
Fingers play the air above the keyboard.
Music rings towards a wail and wanders off.
Another faded day remains,
A crowd of death lays stagnant.

BLUE SPHERE

Two black men are holding hammers.
They violently tear at the door here and on the other edge.
Morning is there; this way their cities can be lined up.
The painter spreads gold on everything.
On the shutters and walls.
The apple orchard is lush with golden apples.
Her blond hair sways there.
In the corner of the yard a sunflower turns, turns, turns and rolls
  its way into the room, becoming a large sphere and sparkling.

The sun is more warm bread than can be carried, and along
  with their homes, we ride the horizon in our attempt to travel
  around the world.

FRAGMENT

The blue officer corps wearing military caps of cloud stands in
    line.
From a bottomless pit they lop off the neck of night.
Sky and trees layer atop one another and seem to be fighting.
The antenna traverses above, running.
Are the flower petals floating in space?
At noon, two suns run up the arena.
The rusty red emotions of summer will soon sever our love.

GLASS WINGS

On the street corner, the sun destroys the love, held between glass
    wings, that people had carefully passed along.
The sky stands facing the window, darkening with every turn of
    the ventilator.
The leaves are in the sky, drawing a single line, as the rooftops
    lean in.
Trains crawl along the bulging street, the sailor's collar rotating
    between blue creases in the sky.
This finely dressed summer procession passes by and crumbles
    into the flask.
The fruits of our hearts rain happy shadows.

CIRCUIT

A fence dirtied by dust continues,
Leaves turn from red to yellow.
Recollections accumulate upon the path of memory. As if
    spreading white linen.
Seasons hold four keys, slip off the stairs. The entrance is shut
    again.
The green tree is hollow. When hit, it sounds.
While night sneaks out.
That day,
I am sad like the skin of the boy in the sky.
Eternity cuts between us.
I lose countless images to that other side.

ILLUSORY HOME

A chef clutches the blue sky. Four fingerprints are left; gradually
  the chicken bleeds. Even here the sun is crushed.
Wardens of the sky who come inquiring. I see daylight take off
  running.
An empty white house where no one lives.
The long dreams of people encircled this house many times, then
  wilted like flower petals.
Death deliberately clings to my finger. Peeling off the shell of
  night, one layer at a time.
This house connects a brilliant road to the distant memory of a
  distant world.

OCEAN OF MEMORY

Hair disheveled, chest splayed out, a madwoman is drifting.
A crowd of white words breaks upon the crepuscular ocean.
A torn accordion,
White horse, and black horse storm across over it, frothing.

BLUE ROAD

The sky, as if after tears.
A tent spread across the land.
The road opens, white, for lovers to pass.

A dye factory!

Dawn stains the skin a rose color.
A flower bouquet atop the cobalt manteau.
Violet eyes sparkle in the dusk,
Crows in mourning attire gather round.
O, when touched, the wall of night crumbles apart.

At any rate, the colors slowly fade each time I cry.

PORTRAIT OF WINTER

The land in the Northern provinces now feels dreary and lethargic. The cities and mountains are all buried in snow with no intention of awakening—slowly, very slowly, they gradually fall deeper into their slumber in this dull, quiet light. The land and sky are blotted out with gray, and the cloudy skies go on for days on end. When the sun is buried in the clouds, a weak light seemingly emitted by the snow itself—a strangely cold, diminished light whose brilliance has faded—creeps in through the window and pours onto a single book atop the desk. It quivers, making spotted shadows here and there. Always impatient, never settling in one spot, it appears to be pulling up the printed letters. All the shadows seem anxious, as if they might disappear in some indistinct manner. Snow accumulates along the slanted roof, and the house lies beyond the gates made of snow. In this naked forest, not a single leaf from the long-forgotten roadside trees makes a move to welcome us. Like a row of brooms, the dead branches stretch higher and higher.

(Azalea, apple, and peaches burst into blossom as if burning up out of the surface of the earth, floating vibrantly into the air) (Kerria flowers line the hedge, and the finely clipped velvet leaves are dyed green by the larch trees) From beneath the thick, dingy layers of snow, who would remember the fact that such things once colored the ground with a gorgeousness dazzling the eyes? These things are kept like a forever-lost memory from a distant world. And in the end they draw rings around only themselves, with assumptions habituated over the decades. Going over the hill I start aging, without even noticing the blinking advertising towers or the overturned green city. And then the pure white snow falls over it. Does the ground know how much effort it takes to awaken, once buried in snow? Everything stops moving—the eyes open just slightly in the dark, then close again. The birds with their wings spread apart, the river ceases to flow. It was like a single long day. Because it was a joy just to discover the clouds moving. The snow falls all day long. Falling straight down from tree to rooftop, or blown along from roof to roof—if one starts snowing, it spreads from one to the next, as if copying each other. The sky spreads low over the ground, rising and falling in tune with some distant ocean. It seems that when the trees supporting the sky can no longer bear the weight of it, that is when the snow falls. It snows so much that no matter how far you push through it, it is impossible to see very far, and such is the kind of snow day where everything disappears, passersby and mountains alike.

Even if at times the sun peeks out through a breach in the sky, the light it casts slowly follows the dead thicket of trees, turning them over like the wind, gradually deepening their color. The road was white like the hallway in my dream. It seems the walls on either side will crumble with every touch. The rows of trees are leaning like shadows. And that figure on the path could possibly be my father. He did not turn around when I called out. In the dark, the snowy road floats up in white—those who go there are not permitted to return. The snow quickly erases the footsteps of many people. Death was nearby. Hiding in the shadows without anyone noticing, and waving its white hand. Death left deep footprints as it passed by. Where are they buried, the bodies of the gentle people. Our lost happiness is hidden somewhere too. This is why the snow-covered ground in the morning is so beautiful. I hear the sound of shoveling, as if digging up our dreams.

Or was it just the wind. I awaken to a sound like a banging on the door. I draw the curtains, and the glass has a white pattern, and snow falls heavily on the other side.

WHITE AND BLACK

The white arrow races by. A bird of night is shot down, dives into
    my pupil.
Incessantly obstructs the sleep of figs.
Silence prefers to pause in the room.
They were candlestick shadows, a pot of torn-off primula,
    mahogany chairs. Time and flames entangle, and I watch over
    them planing the perimeter of the window.
O, the black-faced man comes again today in the rain,
Slaps around the garden in my heart, and runs off.
O rain that comes wearing boots,
Must you trample the earth all the night through.

RIBBON OF MAY

The air roared with laughter outside my window
And in the shadow of its colorful tongue
Leaves are blowing in clumps
I am unable to think
Is there someone there
I reach a hand into the darkness
Only to find   a long wind of hair

MYSTERY

Golden delicious tumbling on the golf course. As if trying not to touch the earth's crust, they dive in spinning. Space starts running in their direction, or the wind gangs up to make a racket. Blue of the cross-section. Hands like the surfacing veins of a leaf. People's hopes will collect like dirt on the side of the road, the way in the past their dreams circled the perimeter of night. Shadows distort, the grass dries up. Two flower petals form a butterfly. They bloom towards morning, filling in the blank earth. We are allowed no predictions for the sake of one day. Just like the trees. And the sky served as window-dressing for everything. When I draw back the curtain a thick fluid gushes forth like water.

Look, the men are getting dizzy again.

OPAL

Pausing in front of the entrance
And peering into the window,
Looking back repeatedly,
The twilight going home.
A sluggish waltz is played by the river.
The sound of clogs beats upon the wall.
Damp air flows past my cheek
And a cloud crosses the puddle.
My vision is about to come to a halt.

DREAM

Reality that disintegrates only in the naked light of day. All ash trees are white bones. She is unable to explain with her back to the clear window. Only her ring replicates its reflection many times over. Gorgeous stained glass windows. The vanities of time. They will detour around the house and choose a street well-trodden. Dark perspiring leaf. The wind above it is crippled and cannot move. Rejecting the illusion of darkness, I come to understand. The faithlessness of people. Outside, the salty air stirs up the spirits.

IN WHITE

Flickering above the grass like a flame
An amethyst button sparkles
And you descend slowly
The turtle dove lends its ear to a lost voice.
A mesh of sunbeams cuts through the treetops.
Green terrace and dried flower petals.
I remember to wind my clock.

GREEN

From the morning balcony   rushing in like a wave
Flooding all over the place
I nearly drown upon a mountain path
And choke, many times bracing myself from falling forward
In my vision, the city opens and closes, spinning like a dream
And in their pursuit, they collapse with tremendous force
I was abandoned

SLEEPING

When the wind where her hair unravels runs down the thicket, it
    becomes a flame.
She brings with her an unbecoming golden ring.
Turning and turning it, she tosses it out into the air.
Much like plants, people hoped to grasp, conquer, and spring back
    against all physical impediments with their entire bodies.
But at the temple the bell does not ring.
For their blue veins were bare, and their backs were the night.
I briefly watched the garden wither at the far end of the sky.
The tree that pulls away from its leaves, like memories discarded.
    That thicket is already gone.
The day is long; decaying lives fill the sunken earth with deep
    crimson.
And then autumn rises from our feet.

THE MAD HOUSE

A bicycle spins.
Along a breezy path in the field.
Only the insides of the rubber wheels exhaust the earth.
He will soon arrive in Baghdad.
It is quite bustling there.
Soldiers of the Red Army, curly-haired artists, pale-skinned
    Ryazan women, the spiral staircase of the cabaret.
The piano makes tinny sounds.
People standing on a mere footprint's worth of dirt are sharpened
    crystals. One wrong step leads to death. The infinite
    propagation of the sun.
At the source of the disease the plants dry up, and the clouds
    tearing through the deteriorated city streets.
Just as the past is nothing for him but an arrangement of trees, it is
    also cold like ash.
The goose feathers at the entrance, the inverted shadow.

I am alive. I thought, I am alive.

SHAPES OF CLOUDS

Pushing through an arch of silver waves,
A procession of people pass through.

Broken-down memories sparkle
Above the rocks, the trees, and the stars.

A wrinkled curtain by the window
Is gathered, then torn apart.

A single garland swaying
In the radiant light made by the city of marble.

Every day, fingertips thin like leaves
Are drawing maps.

WIND

Monotonous words, like a broken gramophone.
The grass opens its bright green mouth and laughs hysterically.
And in that moment the skirts sway quietly.
The road dries up white
And they drag their tired feet
To where the hair flows, red like wolfberries.

DAY OF SNOW

Butterflies flutter daily.
Tearing off the flower patterns from windows
They collect upon the parasol
Spread across your chest.
Reflected in white as they pass by
I chase them   and chase them
But the road is long.

THE DAY THE BELL TOLLS

All day
I hear the fallen, trampled leaves groaning.
Such is the afternoon of life
It reports the time that has already passed.
As when the sound of the bell
Shaves away the flesh of trees
Piece by piece
Because time no longer exists there.

THE CITY POSSESSED

To arouse, anticipate, and hope for
A building, grand with memories
Atop every other ruined thing.
Beauty that constructs our notions in vain
Is at the limits of time—
Their sorrows will never be
Spoken of in their entirety.
However, the ground is of linoleum in full bloom.
A herd of sheep devours the fields and edges of trees
While heavily moving forward
They get pushed up onto the street, falter, and
Continue this exercise.
In winter, all things are
Nothing more than the projection of spirits.
The embracing of spirits,
Tangled like wet yarn.

WAVES

The sailors are laughing.
With their teeth bared,
Like barrel organs
Thrashing in pain all over the place.
Unflaggingly
They press the bellows with their entire bodies
While laughter spreads from shore to shore.

The laughter we have today
Becomes captive to the eternal
And silence only grows deeper still.
For the tongue is simple, like a pair of clappers.
And now, the people
Simply open their mouths
As when yawning.

LIKE A CLOUD

Insects pierce green through the orchard
Crawl the undersides of leaves
Ceaselessly multiplying.
Mucus expelled from nostrils
Seems like blue mist falling.
At times, they
Without a sound flutter and vanish into the sky.
The ladies, always with bleary eyes
Gather the unripe fruit.
The sky has countless scars.
Hanging like elbows.
And then I see
The orchard cleaving from the center.
The skin of the earth emerges there, burning like a cloud.

PLEASE COVER ME WITH DIRT EVERY YEAR

Listlessly walking silently,
Clinging to the honeysuckle on the hedge
Crouched beside the road
O, decrepit old winter—
The hair on your head has dried
And those who walked upon it
Have died too, along with their memories.

TO AWAKEN

Spring descends into the center of our dreams
Scattering roses.
Night burns the bear's pitch black fur
Extends its ruthlessly long tongue
And then the flame, crawling about the earth—

From the singing voice placed
Between lifeless lips
—Soon the celestial flower bouquet
Will open.

TO THE VAST BLOOMING SKY

They are the eyes of everyone.
Are they not the white resonating words.
I'll remove my hat and throw them in.
As the sky and ocean conceal countless flower petals.
One day, at last, blue fish and rose-colored birds will burst through
    my head.
The things I've lost are never to return.

GATE OF SNOW

People's outdated beliefs are piled up around that house.
—Already pale, like gravestones.
Cool in summer, warm in winter.
For a moment I thought flowers had bloomed
But it was just a flock of aging snow.

SIMPLE SCENERY

Cloud-buildings that tremble and sway
Like hopeless drunkards.

I envy the sun that lives in that old garden
Running across the sky.

O—two fighting bulls!
Under your horns, sunlight flows like raging blood.

There, some people wear gilded clothing
And some are blue like the wind.

That territory is, at times,
Just a grave for simple spirits.

Because the daytime is vacant,
The flower petals have already wilted.

And then it is night.
People are in their homes.

Trembling from bewilderment and fear
The darkness that blows in from the infinite.

And again the seeds sparkle all over the world.
Just as the poet sprinkles poems.

SPRING

Flax flowers smell of melting haze.
The violet wisps of smoke are angry feathers.
They fill the fountain of green.
You, the Queen of May,
Will soon arrive.

DANCE HALL

With all of my ears
I listen
As they go back and forth
Their noisy dance steps on the floor
Like mist falling spore-like from the sky
I saw it
The transformation of the flower garden

DARK SUMMER

There was a sycamore outside the window. There was an elm. I watch the air slowly spiral, in the shade of the leaves above my head. They look like they might fall at any moment. They get tangled up like yarn, and the air with thin wings floats through the lace curtains. Like green trimming. Because the light shining through between the black figures collides with the flower petals and thin stems, the carpet of grass is drenched in light, sparkling. That light, as if it had forgotten to get up again, reflects only slightly into the interior. Thus the room was dark and dingy. Everything loses its gravitational center and flees from the interior to the bright outdoors. There, they spin at great speeds. I feel myself gradually getting lighter. My weight was on the tree in the garden. I wonder if that powder on the leaves is dust. The leaves are blown and swaying in the wind, as if unable to withstand their weight on earth. Rubbing the palms of their hands together.

People always pass under the dark damp thicket. Wordlessly, with knees bent, hunched over awkwardly. The streets are silent and the dogs meander along the hedge. The houses have flung open their doors and rooted themselves to the ground. The slate sweats like the black sun in the afternoon. I observe these things absentmindedly. I can't stand this anxiety. Because they are transforming into something completely foreign to me. And they are desperately attached to the bottom of the sky, as if troubled by bad dreams. Only the trees grow by stealing their vitality. The city that has already left me. While I gaze outside, it seems that something invisible lives in my flesh, violating me from the edges, little by little. I turn back again and again. Though my hand is raised, my fingers grasp the edges of my clothes and are convulsing slightly.

What is it that presses down on my head and weighs on me so. Somewhere a crane is rising and falling. Fully loaded with leaves.

When I awakened, the leaves had increased at an incredible rate. They were spilling over. A newspaper was tossed in through the window. I was surprised to see it printed in blue. I am unable to read it. It felt rough to the touch. My eyes always go bad during this season. They get bloodshot, my eyelids swell up. The train commute of my girlhood. The thicket, the woods between the cliffs, enter the train car. The bright green flame that burns its image on both of the glass windows dyes our hands and eyeballs bright blue. The passengers' faces all crumble at once. Divided into dark parts and light parts, they are left smeared on the windows. Leaning against a wall of grass, we leave our textbooks open on our laps and do nothing. I spit out the window. I am now standing and sitting, just like I had done back then. The ophthalmologist peered into my inflamed eye from above a single layer of skin. Scalpel and scissors. Shot of cocaine. I feel the pleasure of these things stimulating me from afar. I am sure that the doctor will remove only the blue part from my retina. Then I will be able to greet people with vigor and walk straight down the street.

I hear a cane tapping the floorboards one by one. There is a tedious loneliness here, ravaged like an abandoned house. It must be a blind person ascending the stairs. This old house makes creaking sounds, like loose floorboards. The old man who appears to enjoy his solitude. That face, always faintly smiling. There was neither despair nor servility there. And then, I saw it yesterday. The man gesturing with his hands as if teaching something by the light of the window. (The blind are always searching for something.) There were countless cabbage worms atop his hands that were like the veins of a leaf. In that moment, the young leaves swaying in the glass were beautiful.

The June sky is immobile. Covered by the shadow of plants grown rampant to the point of depression. The breathing of these creatures crawls up out of the ravine like smoke and flows towards the hill. Pushing through the thicket, it seems there is yet another surface of the earth. Every morning the green surges forward like a flood, overflowing onto the balcony. It carries the blue of the ocean and the smell of grass, and I choke on it. Every time the wind blows, turning over leaves, they rustle like waves. The orchard is awash with apple flowers. Brightly they bloom, drawing boundaries in the sky.

I knew a young boy named Midori. He seemed frail, like the apricot flowers extending their branches from the garden to the roadside. Because he had just come out of the isolation ward. The navy blue smell of his new clothes stings my eyes. Suddenly it grazed my eyes. He is running into the dim orchard. Screaming. It sent animal-like reverberations everywhere. Bare white feet floating in space. In the end the boy never came back.

CONSTELLATION

From a sky wet with dew
From the wide green plains
Awakening
Light is treading above a soft wall
Just barely supported by the dark air of night
As when I was dancing between sleep and death
Everything upon the earth is a shadow of life
And under that grass, our fingers opened like a corolla
A wordless honor   And this madness thrown against the
    glamorous sky
And now, like rocks, they press upon my head.

ANCIENT FLOWERS

Having once bloomed in the ocean breast
But now mostly faded in color
Just as the years arrive from somewhere
And quietly go to ruin
They are already invisible
Young girls collect with their fingertips the lips of the waves
Sounding a hollow ring

ONE OTHER THING

A thicket of asparagus
Dives into the dirty afternoon sun
Their stems cut off by glass
Blue blood streams down the window
And on the other side
Is the sound of a fern unfurling

BACKSIDE

Night eats color
Flower bouquets lose their fake ornaments.
Day falls into the leaves like sparkling fish
And writhes like the lowly mud
The shapeless dreams and trees
Nurtured outside this shriveled, deridable despair
And the space that was chopped down
Tickles the weeds by its feet.
Fingers stained with cigarette tar
Caress the writhing darkness.
And the people move forward.

BLEMISH ON THE GRAPE

In the afternoon rocking chair, cloud-covered eyes gaze at the
    black specks darting through the air.
A branch loaded with leaves rises solemnly to the sky, leaving
    behind teeth marks.
Now, as ever, are the stemless flowers which once grazed the
    darkness of my eyelids burying the deformed streets of the
    northern lands.
The pure thoughts and shadows which autumn crushes.
My flesh, while trampling quietly upon them in the corner of the
    yard, watches over the whereabouts of that which is destroyed.
As wings circling under the trees turn into their helpless coffin.

The juice of the crushed grapes
Stain the sky, and darkness is dampened by the air.
Lingering in the pallid dusk
The people hang their heavy hearts to dry.

SNOW LINE

Faded, worn-down time scatters into the air as ardent seeds. Leap over silent forms, and wash away the artificial rouge of technique from the lips, which bleed blooming flowers every time you traverse the earth!

Having discarded yesterday's wind, the branch that firmly shakes the hand overflowing with promises changes passion and hope into powerless figures. The accumulation of thought left behind for those who have lost their steps to the relentless attack of those corpses. The glory filling the heart of the traveler crossing this parched sandbank is already lost, and an unfamiliar shard of snow melts into the night. What is it that keeps dragging me into the endgame.

PROMENADE

Seasons change their gloves
The three o'clock
Trace of sun
Of flower petals that bury the pavement
A black and white screen
Eyes are covered by clouds
Evening sets on some promiseless day.

CONVERSATION

—The hand of God shall be raised for the sake of the seasons buried under a heavy rhythm. The rail line crawling out of the undulating waves bloom with salt flowers. Yearning for the biorhythms of all things, the antique keyboard with its dusty fingers awaits a sun-ripened moment.

—Leave dreams to the dreamers. Amidst the grass, the heat haze makes those green tentacles flutter, protecting their easily torn shadows. Moreover, the purple smoke of the madrigal turns the sky to frosted glass.

—I hear the sound of a leaf bud tearing. Sweet fruit of a great joy. The flow of a pace that strikes people in the retina.

—Already lost and returned to the earth under a pitch-black gravestone, endless colors seek to know when it is time to dishevel reality and flower gardens alike.

—

—Turning into a battle cry for those who awaken repeatedly while tumbling around the eternal abyss, that sound gives birth to me, and that light shoots me through. The hotel lobby is buried in saffron to properly welcome this feast from heaven.

LATE GATHERING

I whistle and they come back from deep in the sky. So that there is no chance of drowning in the endless colors. Emerald, ruby, and diamond flower petals drenched in a new brilliance roam the fields and mountains. Thin drooping folds of grass send out the slightest breeze. The terrace opens out to the sea, and countless damp conversations spill out. No longer, but at times vividly.

CLIMBING TO HEAVEN

There are socks drying in the station
Hanging from a yurika branch
A fickle wind prays to the thicket
Clouds in the shade of saplings are trampled
And a group of stars migrates to the north
Countless times, winter sets tombstones in the earth
And the rose decorating that chest is burned-out ash
Passion, as it eventually declines
Will report on their absence
And the moonlight in their eyes
Remains absolutely useless.

MAYFLOWER

Full bloom inside the piano
I touch it and the keys begin to move
The impudent grass is food for the calves
Lilas flowers make a crown
Spanish money descends
Between the plants of glass

DARK SONG

Upon the new carpet all abloom
Quietly slowly
Two donkeys push a lorry.
On the street where the proud flower petals burn
Silk feathers are stained by pollen.
And where her toes touch
A white rainbow is portrayed.

AFTERNOON OF FRUIT

Rain drove off the leaves from the trees
The village has no need for music   for the cadence of their
brilliant shadows pounding the ivory keys and the dark earth, not
    even if their trees went naked.
Already the finale is on the roughened grass,
The bruised fruit are scattered atop the hill.

FLOWER

Dreams are severed fruit
Auburn pears have fallen in the field
Parsley blooms on the plate
Sometimes the leghorn appears to have six toes
I crack an egg and the moon comes out

AFTERNOON

Rains like flower petals.
Hit by a heavy weight, insects descend the tree shade.
Gathering at the mast wall, trailing a faint breeze—sounds are
    killed by the sun, the waves.
My skeleton places white flowers upon it.
Interrupted by thoughts, fish climb the cliff.

MEERSCHAUM

The spotted air grows heavy, the *ventilator* blows leaves into the sky.

There is a blizzard on the ocean, its purpose to pile layers of flower petals like paper scraps, and then to bury their unfocused music in the pavement. Dried up clouds are pasted on the other side of the display window.

To the nodding grass, the *lantern* shadows, and then onto a deep slumber—somewhere, cicadas unravel ferns.

As a lump of rotten air leaves behind an indecipherable scream, and as the fervent desires of these old-fashioned ones hoping to return again—as well as the echoes of the dark summer—wander the spaces between the tips of branches, a distant hour is lost, and then, to think that it should shine above us after all.

END OF SUMMER

August, and the leaves have died off early
The sun crawls over the charred hill
There, the rhythms of nature simply help the trees converse
But in the city, forgotten sounds contemplate the colors and
    shapes of waves
As always, stars are abloom at the ranch
The swarming of which the cows eat in the shape of an arch
Coming in from the frozen port, an invisible season
As well as everyone's day, are about to come to an end

FINALE

Behind me, an old person sings of a cracked heart, and of the sun
The effect of which collides into a thin wall of ebonite
And is likely to never end
Honeybees were buried in an abundance of fennel pollen
Summer was no longer nearby
Deep in the woods a tree is felled
Attenuated time comes quickly at first, then gently passes by
So as not to fall behind
Leaving brown footprints in the withered field
All earthly marriage ceremonies have come to an end

A PLAIN, MOONLIT NIGHT

A butterfly landed on the pipe organ on the rooftop garden
The unseasonable syllables wrench the lady's heart
The bouquet is torn away   the fire does not burn
Outside the window a deer passes by, trampling on the stars
At the ocean bottom, fish mock the weather   people put on their
    glasses
This year, too, the widowed moon deceives its age

PRELUDE

Out of sight and covered by clouds, the leaves multiply with incredible vigor. Without warning they are carried in, the sycamore and zelkova trees filling up with new leaves—like wriggling creatures they well up and overflow, sparkling. From a distance, I see the air suddenly pull together, the black clusters overlapping to create darkness. Then it gradually expands towards the hill and seems to turn into a thicket, though it is unclear whether there really is a thicket or if it is a row of trees. At times, the sky is so high and distant, you would think it got so dirty because it was injured by something. The hollow below is a field, youthful like the breast of a pigeon, and the ladies from the city exclaim in surprise, *Why, it's just like the Gulf of Spada.* And they sit on their picnic blankets eating sandwiches and chocolates, discussing the lovely weather, and how organdy butterflies are going to be fashionable this summer. All this time, the green fountain rotates ceaselessly, glowing like newspapers being spit out of the rotary press.

It makes me dizzy to know how varied are the repeating lives of the endless morning plants. There are no human footsteps, nor the smell of butter or cheese, but nonetheless as I watch over their stifling propagation and battle and exultation, I am on the brink of losing. Outside our home, yet so near to us, they align their footsteps as if to threaten, moaning in inexplicable gloom, forcing me to keep watch outside. I wonder how long it has been since I have been dragged in and ensnared by such surroundings. The only things I can see without cacophony or deception, aside from the air and sky and trees and grass, are their flowing colors and rough, lurid shapes. With a strange intensity, they push me out the door, making me sad, making me angry.

When I slowly open my eyes, as if goaded into it, close to my eyelids there is a simple exchange of greetings with nature. I feel that I have awakened. Then the ceiling stained yellow from the leaking rain, and the walls covered with little nail holes, gradually become absorbed by the weak violet light trying to awaken from sleep, receding further and further away. I feel I have lost something I should not have allowed to escape. Just like when a child clings to the hopes of being reunited with some lost object. Even as I consider recapturing it, it is only tepid like warm water, there is nothing that returns. As my upper body suddenly grows lighter, I am unable to remember anything, and there is no longer any appeal in the fact of its passing. And then the woods and sun and fence appear vividly as if they were left behind from an early morning dream.

Those nearby will probably continue their usual, gentle repetitions. These clustered shapes of plants should have nothing to do with me, but somehow I feel the need to be cautious of each and every one, as if I am bound to them. I grow drowsy watching over the moving tips of treetops, and every day as I mumble to myself, the day comes to an end.

The elm tree in the center of the garden spreads its stiff branches like a wedding veil, and at the foot of the tree, weeds surround it like the teeth of a saw. The spots that differentiate the unkempt grass—dahlias, columbines, white nettle, rushes and such—spin around like celluloid toys. That's right, placed atop the tangled mesh, space is unable to detach and fall away from the leafy veins. I ponder how the small activity of ants going back and forth between the stems of grasses occupies most of that space. Was there such a dark, narrow road here—unnoticed by humans, there is this constant business of living by walking across the wires that would disappear into thin air at the slightest touch; if the chestnut flowers should happen to cluster and fall, the less visible insects would likewise move on to the next stalk time and time again. What are you thinking, and where are you going—regardless of how insignificant your beginnings may have been, try not to lose hope before determining your direction.

Seasons, returning without a doubt and without any error in their path, and traveling around the world without any warning—when they burst forth with countless sprouted seeds, how we had desired the exuberant construction of plants. With similar speed, the plants share their short feathers with all the fields in this world of avarice, leading people to look in different directions. Because our usual field of vision had been replaced by something unfamiliar before anyone could notice, we came to crave the intensity of color and freedom.

I see the day break through the shaggy, kinky green gates. The dawn that comes from the depths of the atmosphere, flowing gently like the clearing mist, is a beautiful labyrinth. People tend to have unseemly thoughts when they encounter that which is too beautiful. Something bad must have happened while we were sleeping. It appears calm on the surface but only because it conceals a secret, this quiet brimming with eerie uncertainty. If I don't scream soon I might be killed. Why not rebel, steeped in this stagnant air. We are possessed by humid air rising from thick grass that suffocates and confines us, and yet the plants steal all vitality away from humans, staging a banquet without end.

I believed at once that trees have blue blood running through them. Because they speak in such a prophet-like manner. Because the sap leaves small stains on our skin and muscles, my hands swell up, my heart about to tear from the cold. On farms in the Northern country, it is said that wheat must be quickly harvested and dried, lest the calves come tearing through the fence, and also that wool scarves should be prepared. Soon the snow will come and freeze over the trees.

My friends have started to plan their days around the patterns in the sky and colors of flowers. They worry about the state of the weather, measuring warmth or coldness at the tips of their fingernails. They believe in some kind of promise, or communication, between the color of their clothes or lipstick, for example, or even the placement of furniture, with the scene outside their windows. They believe that they are controlled by these subtle gradations, and feel the need to constantly be in harmony with the landscape. At times they try to bloom more beautifully than a flower. This is why, as they gaze at the colors of flower petals, or watch the growth of a tree, their skin and their movements are changing all of their own accord.

The plants, abundant with change, grow so vigorously that I am no longer able to read books or smoke cigarettes. In an attempt to not miss the slightest movement in their expressions—their branches are swaying, they are fiercely surrounded—my own expressiveness becomes something quite useless. Even raising my hand, or laughing, is nothing but a precise imitation of their expressions. There is not a single thing that is mine, I am simply repeating their movements, stealing their expressions. I can no longer tell which is the shadow of which. There is nothing that I have given them. And yet I have accepted everything they do. Sooner or later I shall transform into a tree and disappear into their fold. All this time I had believed I was alive, and yet perhaps I do not even exist. The mere shadow of a tree, the ghost-like figure that crawls on the ground only in the afternoon—these too will soon grow invisible. Eventually, the wisdom of the trees will pass up and above our heads. People will lose equilibrium, bracing themselves, and stagger forward, pressing their hats against their heads. I learned that the ardor I had long bestowed upon humanity was of little account; it was like the time I regretted the injury to my scratched up finger that scraped only shards of glass.

Even as all the faces and incidents have been forgotten, the first memories to emerge, after all, are the forms of nature, like the shape of a mountain or the size of a tree—and then, like spinning yarn, various events, buildings, food and such are drawn out, and humans only peek in from between, in a confused mess, and then turn into a languishing memory. If the past is to be thrown away like a worn-out piece of air, I wonder what kind of conversation would be the most comforting to the aged. The reason why people look back into the fading distance until their scars shine with brilliance is because we hold in our hearts the belief that our youthful adolescence lies in the direction where the flowers are blooming.

The rain washes the trees all day, and the duet with the earth begins. Out of nowhere, or in bits and pieces, a rhythmical wave surges forward, coloring the plants in reds and yellows. The cheerful music that we desire and arrest seems to be quickening the seasons by quite a bit. I could no longer make out the voices. Autumn has only just begun, but there are coals in the stove, and all the family has come out to the balcony to listen to the simple tune played by invisible strings. A branch like a steel frame hangs down from the sky, and the sunshade fabric is removed. The elm tree is now naked. The time here seems to pass in the direction of the leaves falling. In their hearts, everyone laments their age. Because one ring is a souvenir of a lively day, but also becomes a chain tying us to the past. All that has faded scatters in the sky, waiting for the final cadence. The empty echoes approaching gradually—they wander among trees like desolate melodies. The changing of nature, and the regulated order—do they hope for glorious dreams upon the lips.

SEASONS

September, and the leaves have died off early
The sun crawls along the hill, scorched raw
There, the rhythms of nature simply help the trees converse

But in the city, forgotten sounds contemplate the colors and
    shapes of waves

As always, stars are abloom at the ranch
The swarming of which the cows eat in the shape of an arch

Coming in from the frozen port, an invisible season
As well as the entirety, this heart's day, are all about to end

WORDS

Mother spoke as if in song

Those old stories can still melt the ice on our chests

The ocean swells in the lower regions of winter burning with a
small noise   ringing golden dreams   and submerging
countless mumblings

Deception and ruin, resembling fallen leaves, will soon block the
road

There is no more tomorrow   people are simply tired

Demeaned   in the distance a twisted wind dries out the snow and
in this way, here

Only the betrayed words devour idleness to no end

Waiting for that final, unrecognized hour

DOWNFALL

—Listen: to the sprouts emerging from within the hurricane.
The garden is now trying to go to ruin.
Will the wind that extinguishes trembling life   again relieve its
    burden on the trees.
The trunks of arrogance and laziness chopped down to the earth
    brutally torment your thinking.
They are all forms of deception   provisional, painted masks.
The ocean of the blazing sun opens   entangles with a field of
    roses   only the spoken words beg forgiveness   while trying
    to live.

COMPOSITION IN THREE PRIMARY COLORS

The post office is a mile away.

In front of the butcher shop, a leghorn bends its beak scrounging for feed. Locally grown eggs for sale, it says on the window. A man in a white apron sneezes, with a knife gleaming between the tendons of the beast. Passing by the rear gates of the elementary school, there is a commotion like a swarm of bees, and the national anthem departs from the keys of the organ, one octave lower. When they arrive at a distant wind-like conclusion, the village is completely submerged into the air, and the birds no longer sing in this region of calm. The nandina field is viscous and beautiful like melted lacquer. I see an army fleet on a hill; it is round like a bun of scorched, dead grass. On a sunny day, a brown lizard watches the ventilation tube spin around, *kerakerakerakera*. What is that! Rows of boots with freshly applied cream. Singing out of tune, I walk down a street with a cedar forest and a bamboo grove and a clothes-drying rack. The soldiers say that the fruit atop the donkey's back is funny. Which reminds me that the sun is a cheap, gleaming thing that at first shines near the eyes, then slips back and follows people around all day—but it seems to have grown a bit distorted. There is a mental hospital in the middle of the field. They say the flag on the rooftop is a landmark so that people won't get lost. From the balcony I see the laundry person's bike detouring around it on its way here. Further above the rooftop where the saffron has bloomed all over, silk slippers are raining down. The river close to my ears always shows me such dreams. Music with loosened strings bursts out through a rift in a boring moment. To anticipate a lighthearted letter on a Sunday afternoon is enjoyable like the feeling of loving the rhythms of a ribbon being teased by the wind, atop the head of a doe. It is also amusing to consider those white thorns touching the heart. The naked trees can be seen transparently into the depths of the sky. A man wearing a wool coat over a blue kimono is up on a tree stump, using his umbrella as a cane, swaggering in front of all the children and adults that surround him. "YOU CRAZY FOOLS. DO YOU, DO YOU KNOW WHEN THIS ROAD WAS BUILT? HOW OLD THIS ZELKOVA TREE IS? I, I, DURING THE PROSPEROUS TIMES OF 1917, YES, IF I HADN'T LOST IT ON THE MARKET, I WASN'T ASKING YOU IF NAPOLEON HAD COME TO CAUCASUS. MY YOUNGER BROTHER HAD TWO THOUSAND HECTARES OF FARMLAND. AND YET THE RICE IS EXPENSIVE. DON'T YOU LAUGH NOW—ANY MOMENT NOW YOU'RE GOING TO STUMBLE. HA HA HA HA HA. . . ." What a cold outcry. His toothless mouth was inflamed and bright red. Let's quickly shut the windows of the cakebox-like hospital across the way—there is an evil wind blowing from over there. A cold that invades the brains of young people. We don't make much of an exception for running in order to catch the train.

OCEAN BRIDE

I do awaken to the sound of the wind snaking through a dark
    ocean of trees.
Beyond the gray skies
The cuckoo cries out,
Kefukaero, kefukaero—
To where shall I return.
In order to get to the tail end of noon,
The thicket of gooseberry and knotweed was quite deep.
The apples, in my half-faded memory,
Were in full bloom.
And the invisible screams, too.

If I rush past the damp windbreak path
I shall arrive at the dunes with the sorrels and wild strawberries.
They shine like jewels and are lovely to eat.
The ocean froths
And is spreading its lace.
The short train is headed for the city.
Alienated by the evil gods
Time alone, layered on the lip of the wave, is dazzling.
From there I await someone's words
And hear a song pressing up towards reality.
Now is the time that people, like parasols,
Try to enter the banquet of trees covering the earth.

SONG OF THE SUN

A white body
Whirling in the searing wind
Kneels down in a shorn-off darkness
The beasts grown weary of sunlight and pleasure
Howl at a substitute for night
Because Dante's Inferno does not exist there
But the old instruments have stopped playing
In the mirror of diamonds, the snow
Curves
Spreading its wings like the light
And then the veil
Conceals the music of the tattered air
And a voiceless season on some shore
Will radiate in youth and honor

MOUNTAIN RANGE

Distant peaks swaying like the wind
In the orchard at the mountain base, bright white flowers bloom
Paused in mid-winter, the hillside
Is beautiful like a spread of silk over every morning
Water flows noisily through my eyes
And I wish to bow down in gratitude—*thank you*—to an invisible
 being
But no one is listening   there is no forgiveness
Will the turtle dove cry in sympathy
And echo my voice back to me

The snow will disappear
And laurel flowers and red lilies will bloom in the valley
Creating a covering of green
In the nettles, too, the slow summer will lurk
And in our hearts
How beautiful the flames that will flare up in a ring

OCEAN ANGEL

The cradle rings loudly.
A spray shoots up,
As if tearing off feathers.
I wait for the return of those able to sleep.
Music marks the bright hour.
I try to complain, raising my voice—
The waves come erase it from behind.

I was abandoned in the ocean.

VOICES OF SUMMER

It looks far   very far
Wrapped in a thick wool manteau
It is purple like the fog
Saburo! Saburo!   she yells
His mother awaiting reply
Above the deep slumber of summer
A lizard faces the wind

It looks near   very near
Heavy knees have begun to move
On the edge of town the adults fret over the weather
And fuss about
Crouching, fallen silent,
Making us gossip all day long
When split, the water flows like pollen

SEASONAL NIGHT

Loaded with young green leaves
The last train of the light rail goes by
Quietly, like the back alley of the season.
It crawls along like a snail
Through the larch forest and to the cabbage fields.
Those with no business here should go ahead and disembark.
Six leagues to the dye factory deep in the woods.
Gleaming upon the dark evening road,
A trickle of sap.

THE STREET FAIR

A cloud has collapsed on the pavement
Like the horse's white struggle for air

Night, screaming and shouting into the darkness
Arrives with the intention of murdering time

Wearing a mask plated with light beams
Lining up single-file from the window

People moan in their dreams
And fall from sleep to an even deeper sleep

There, a stem that has gone pale
Like an exhausted despair

Supports the tall sky
An empty city with neither roads nor stars

My thinking is to escape
That pitch-black metal house

Steal away the glimmer of pistons
And smoldering embers of noise

Retreat into a shallow ocean
Collide, get battered to the ground

1.2.3.4.5.

Under a row of trees a young girl raises her green hand.
Surprised by her plant-like skin, she looks, and eventually
  removes her silk gloves.

NEWLY COLLECTED POEMS

FALLING OCEAN

A red riot takes place.

In the early evening the sun dies alongside the ocean. The waves are unable to catch the clothes that float away after them.

The ocean builds a blue road from the vicinity of my eyes. Countless gorgeous corpses are buried below it. Annihilation of a band of tired women. There is a boat that hurriedly covers its tracks.

There is nothing that lives there.

TREE SPIRITS

Through the tunnel in the woods, following the telegraph line that
   stretches to the foot of the mountain
Once again a childhood memory comes back to me
The valley is dark, and it is cold
O wandering voice
You were right there
Twilight chasing the merchants who cross the streets of melting
   snow
A swarm of mosquitos circles higher and higher under the eaves

Ah—won't you return. Right away
In the form of joyful cries. Deepening the melancholy of the boy's
   day that shakes the mountains and seeps into the distant sky, all
   traces of people fade into the distance

FLOWER

1

Dreams are severed fruit
Auburn pears have fallen in the field
Parsley blooms on the plate
Sometimes the leghorn appears to have six toes
I crack an egg and the moon comes out

2

A snail crawls through the forest
Above its tentacles is the sky

3

The color of the wind is dark today
The piston charges ahead, breaking through the salty air
Rain turns to sand under the overturned morning

FLOWERS BETWEEN THE FINGERS

1

Walking along the back alley of the hotel yesterday, I spotted some yellow flowers growing just below the guardrails. A single dab of color on the dry dirt between the cracks in the asphalt.

The long line connected through the reflection of the bright afternoon pavement on the body of the car is beautiful. Many times I have wanted to chase after it. I thought I would find the sun there. The sound of the engine and the smell of oil fill the city with a buoyant air, rattling windows on both sides. On the street corner a crane hoists iron beams up into the air. I hope that it doesn't damage the thin air. The sound of things breaking, and the allure of a continuously dynamic space, are wonderful. Because I keep staring at the beauty of the jagged cross-section, I am perhaps only tiring out my eyes.

2

Begonias call up the image of Chinese women's shoes. Small, lush, peach-colored flower petals dampen in the frame of a just-opened set of curtains.

Under a row of trees a young girl raises her green hand, calling someone. Looking in surprise at her plant-like skin, she eventually removes her gloves.

3

Late at night, a hammer in the shape of a human digs into the earth's crust by the light of a small lantern. And tries to lead us to the other side of a pitch black hole. Any moment now there will come a time when we can forget the bright ground above. The destruction and construction of the land—these are the kinds of things by which humans are defeated.

4

A horse comes neighing up the hill. The breath exhaled from his nostrils were stark white clouds. He comes tearing through the street where the milk flows. I had thought that the flowers had bloomed in the fields.

5

In the cabbage field in the morning, drops of dew collect under large leaves, but most of these become the main diet of insects. Cabbageworms have such translucent bodies because they feed on gems of dew.

6

In a crystal vase, a single kensis stem grows. The liquid lead is toxic. When I read books, I remove my glasses and place them nearby.

LAVENDER GRAVE

All the keys have left the piano
I shall drown my joys into the pitch black wilderness.
Exposed chords of the air that obstruct
The naked parade of afternoon shall be severed.
Rhythmical waves long for the festival that has passed.
The loud laughter of the spirits, as if praying forever,
Prod the branches to take a bow
And blow out our activities.
The destruction of those giants
Will soon set the frozen marble into the earth.

SMOKE SIGNALS

Beating the golden tendon
In the light from the blue sky
The daughter of the sun
Applauds the new sacrificial ritual.
The morning plays
Upon the keys of the harpsichord.
Dirty ivory fingers are scrabbled together
And as life is burned
The time has come to spring into action.

NIGHT WALK

Deep in the night the pavement runs dry, crude as if covered in lead, green phlegm spit out everywhere. These raw globs conjure up the flower-like parts of the exposed, dirty, rotten organs of humans, driving me towards an elusive, eerie sensation. The people who by day conceal all they have to hide with their artful expressions and unctuous conversations must be the same ones who are relieved to abandon only the most monstrous parts of themselves throughout this darkness, among the newspaper scraps and orange peels. Bearing down on them with the teeth of their *geta* sandals, kicking them with their toes, men and women alike fled from these city streets at night. Then the commotion comes to a complete halt and it again falls silent as if nothing had happened. There are no dog eyeballs to flick away, and all shadow-like shadows sink into a plausible destruction, darkness licking its lips. What I fear are the tentacles of darkness that will completely do me in. Their inarticulate blades that melt my partially frozen heart with an invisible force, or simply abandon me at some point with no promises at all.

I walk on now. I consider how it was only these filthy residues that filled in reality while collecting the empty shells discarded by strangers, and how the beautiful feathers I had always believed permeated the blank spaces lay just above a muddy, undependable swamp. It seems as if that dizzying moment when arrogant personalities, buildings, and sounds filter through reality has just now taken place, but it might actually be an event from the distant past. A single drop of black water dripping from the mouth of a feeble bottle is pushed forth by night, which is made of something akin to the wall we lean on. It passes under the colonial harbor and flows through the hearts of those who have been betrayed—it is probably not possible to stem this flow until it grows light.

The windows of the houses on either side no longer flutter. They shut their entrances like mimosas as I pass by. Many eyes peek out of the cracks in the doors, and returning to the chatting they had just finished, they badmouth me, laughing at my peculiarities and spreading rumors. The sounds that leak out from within these quiet mumblings give me halt. They are after me. I am not permitted to turn back. Up ahead, the train tracks curve in the air, giving off brilliant sparks. I am merely running in place in a small circle, troubled by the soles of my feet that are sticky as if straddling a bumpy map. In terms of where I stand, I am only supported by the part of the ground where the heels of my shoes barely touch, and there is no extra space anywhere else. It is extremely difficult to walk with the instability of shackles. We repeatedly see the illusion of being shoved into a deep ravine. I cling to a piece of yarn, to a honeysuckle hedge. The electric crown that lights only our feet passes by, sneering at the people and distorting the faces of the apathetic men. As if to say, *you're hopeless, there's nothing more for you to do.* It would be plenty just to scoop up their cruel words and loud laughter.

Not that anyone is looking, but I shudder as if I was naked. There were no leaves on the roadside trees. I think my retina will tear at the touch. The arm of the monster that has held me captive until now is relentlessly coercive. It tries to make me believe, or to spoil my heart with sweetness. It is a deception that has just completed its intangible construction. It is a cruel lashing for the innocent woman forever trying to dredge up what she has lost. That is why we no longer hear the elegant echoes. Because the scent of ripened sunlight was not there either. Even as the internal organs of the internal organs are heaved out and torn to shreds, the voice separated from the flesh will get tossed out into the winter day, leaving behind its ugly skeleton.

I had longed to be overcome by a storm of freedom and

love. But those ties were broken. Already the clearness of spirit has been lost, and the earth is fatigued, barely able to handle the weight of its load. It repeats the low-pitched sounds with an irritated look. The flash of light that sparks on occasion was the only coquetry towards tomorrow I could see.

I stir up some back alley face powder, count the coins in the palm of my hand, and the twelve-twenty-eight wind blows. The wind that traverses day and night takes me by both hands and begins to run. A film-like ocean floats up from between those swaying walls. On the dark surface of the sea where no amount of snow will collect, in a corner where no flowers bloom, where there is no slippage like in the city where I walk, a team of waves hiding some vacant disturbance calls back some nearly-destroyed memory, rushes forth at once and narrows the field of vision while imparting a damp, mica-like sparkle. That mournful outward appearance will lament. The wound is exposed—until it disappears while adding life to the fault lines of thought.

I try to turn the corner. Who would ever try to put down roots in such a dank region. Forget the murmuring of the stars. The flower petals overhead that fall in time with the pistons that stitch the flank of night are shimmering. A single man with a kerchief around his neck huddles under the eaves, peeking out at the sky as if he had just recently descended to earth. His strangely ancient expression and muddy veins are transparent. A monologue spills out from between his teeth—*I have to hurry home, it's time to go home.*

LARKS OF THE FLOWER GARDEN

Scene I

Figures of love
Vividly drawn on the city pavement.
Lilac flowers in the lobby of the sky
Opened the dark day inside the eyes
Into black and white.

Scene II

The voices of girls singing in chorus from the Easter lily
Are first to tear through the season.
When the oats headed for the colonies
Sprout atop the freight ship
The penguin shakes its apron
From the shadows of the clouds of the dining table.
Shells
Butterflies
Oh!

WIND IS BLOWING

Swaying as if in the wake of
A gaily laughing procession
Through the dark garden,
To whom do these trees try to speak.

Drying out my daydreams
Like a distant voice,
Invisible footsteps
Trample on my shadow
On the ice.

Outside, the afternoon
Was violently extinguished.
The seagull twisted its bill
To gather warm words
From the swarms of waves,
And escaped into the lantern.

The people wait for spring,
In search of lost time.
They will wish for the seagull
To once again return to their eyes.

SEASONS

One clear day
Along the mountain pass
The horse felt like having a smoke.
A nightingale is singing
While sewing the clouds stitch by stitch.
It struck a sad note
Of a happiness that passed by without having come to it.
The deep green mountains fell silent
And blocked the path.
Out of sadness, he gave a single high-pitched neigh.
His mane, long like dead grass, burned
And the same scream could be heard from elsewhere.

Now the horse felt the presence of something warm nearby.
And saw the distant years and months dissipate in an instant.

PROSE

NOTABLE POEMS FROM THE SECOND YEAR
OF PUBLICATIONS IN *SHII NO KI*

Of the poems published in *Shii no ki* in 1933, the following two I found to be the most remarkable.

- "Morning Pipe" by Ema Shōko
  A fresh poem.

- "One who is alone" by Yamanaka Fumiko
  I found it to be a very strong work.

WHILE WAITING FOR CHRISTMAS

★

Clever ladies always press their lips up to the window of the cake shop, gazing at the decorated sweets and exclaiming, *Oh! How beautiful!*—but they have not once claimed to want to eat them. 'Tis the season for tea and sweets again. Yellows and reds, or perhaps whites and purples—look how they fill in both sides of the street so beautifully, like blooming flowers.

Speaking of flowers, which do you prefer? In order to keep you from drowning in the endless colors that surround you. For an evening party, I definitely recommend these fragrant orchids. Fake flowers on the chest are so passé. Now where can I find a sassy young woman who would jump out of a restaurant with a black beret angled down her forehead, a tiny tiny yellow chrysanthemum pressed under it? That fresh flower that goes so well with this season, that dress in that moment, now that's what you should consider your personal emblem. Don't you just love the charm of tossing a wilted crumpled red flower out the car window late at night? Okay goodbye.

WINTER DIARY

December [—]

It's been a while since I've seen either the mountains or the ocean. I wish I could go to the mountains. When the wind blows, I feel like abandoning everything and going home. I think I can hear the tides of the pitch black northern ocean. Or am I just hearing the sound of trains—no, it is the tide.

I now long for the piles of seashells I used to own. The ones I collected in an empty cigar box, over a long time. Red ones, shiny ones, round ones, pointy ones—though I've already given them all away.

I can't stand this intense nostalgia I feel for the ocean—like I could just slip back a few years in time. The tide that sounds like the rising and falling of the earth itself. White, cresting waves pushing forward, the residual dampness as they recede, the roughening, the endless banging sound, the spray gathering like a heavy mist, filling up the beach. The ocean that goes crazy in the corner of a city buried in snow, immobile like the dead. As if I might just pack up my things and head home tomorrow, to the home that sounds of the ocean—I walk along the city like this, remembering the ocean.

I've had enough of walking these crowded streets. The pavement filled with fur coats, overcoats, display windows and peals of laughter, it's all a bit too glamorous for me. I finally finished proofreading *Esprit*. I think it will be an interesting journal. I wonder if it will sell. Scraps of paper and dead brown leaves are all tossed about by the wind, and indeed it is getting to be that time now, for the city to grow just a little bit dingy.

December [—]

I warmed my cold hands by the electric lamp. And realized they were very pretty. My red fingers with bloated blood vessels under pale skin. As I opened and closed them, they bloomed beautifully like the fused corolla of a flower. I thought I should take good care of them.

I am always admiring and longing for the flowers of others—in other people's gardens, in flower shops.

I stay up late reading biographies of Western musicians. All these great people. It's fascinating, like reading fairy tales.

CHAMBER MUSIC

★

The pavement is frozen solid and the winter streets feel rather dull, but these women find joy in drawing vibrant figures of love as if gliding across an ice rink.

When you are *avec* your lover, do you walk on his left or his right side. In either case, the more you believe in him, the more you should walk on the display window side. When you're bored, and also when you're not, there is nothing more sensible than that. But when you're all alone, walk as quickly as possible. Thoroughly inspecting those display windows is such a silly waste of time.

When it's cold out, there is something so seemingly pleasant about that steamy interior, particularly that of a restaurant or café. Although these places are usually rife with toxic conversation and negative energy. Those must be the times when you feel a little pang of hunger. When you do, prepare to return right away to your suburban home. And when you grow tired of staring out at the suburban scenery as you're jostled on the bus or train, and the people seated across from you all seem as boring as robots, please feel free to take a peek at this journal called *Esprit*. Under that dim, economical light of the lamp, may it sparkle before you like a fresh, elegant, or effective jewel. May it act at times like a lighthearted friend, or adorn like a flower each and every joyful life of the *ladies and gentlemen*, in the hopes that it will become a fountain of knowledge that does not need to be concocted.

O fickle friends! Having tired of sports, movies, and even the games of love, if you had any intention to follow the urban fashions that shift like the eyes of a cat, I do suggest giving this handy, portable little travel guide a try.

CRYSTAL NIGHT

Abe-san writes poetry on glass. Under the sun, they should become sparkling, fairytale-like fragments. And then they bloom one at a time into transparent flower petals, so as to decorate the Grecian night. When these controlled, jewel-like flower petals shimmer in the breast of night, they are so dazzling that I close my eyes. Then, in the darkness behind my eyelids, I see a beautiful arrangement of shadows.

It might cut my fingers to touch them.

Sometimes I try to scratch up the glass, but my finger only skids across the surface.

The misfortune in Abe-san's poetry is, in fact, that it is not printed with lead type upon paper.

The secret within this multifaceted glass is indeed the dawn where 19th-century poems get crushed in the palm of the hand.

HAD THEY BEEN THE EYES OF FISH

Whenever I get bored I look at paintings. It is there that I see people's hearts in various flower petal shapes, or discolored into sad yellows and purples, all of it on display. A horse wearing glasses comes tearing down the barren, pitch black mountain. It's all very amusing because I have never before seen a living heart nor dead skin. What gorgeous poetry! And here I was only trying to draw words like insect crawlings on a dry scrap of paper. Beautiful spots of color fill in the parts that are the wind and the ocean. The dreams of the artist are completely stained with pigment, still vividly wet. I had dismissed them as mere scribblings, but seeing those internal organs torn to shreds and shimmering, I shudder with pleasure. Leaping rhythms, undulating air. There is something attractive about this diverse life painting on the wall, rotating in front of my eyes.

A painter is a master of lines and colors with which to freely embody an image of a moment in a real space. His alchemy succeeded in destroying all mundane notions. Quite boldly he constructs the images thoroughly analyzed by the light of the sun and the internal spirit. There were times when he gave shape to that which had not even occurred to people. Or, shattering that which we had grown familiar with and bored of, assigning them new labels with new values. I believe that the work of a painter is very similar to that of a poet. I know this because looking at paintings wears me out. Though I doubt there are many poems that are written with the same attention to the effect of color- or motif-based composition, the mood engendered by shadows, and lines determining their point of contact with space within a composition. I suspect that most poems are written with whatever random thought occurs to the poet. In some cases that's fine, although poems like that are already ruined. They are banal and have a short life span.

When painting a single apple, I do not think we should attribute the concept of roundness or redness to the object. Because the very arbitrarily defined common knowledge regarding this single sphere called an apple has no application whatsoever in terms of paintings. Even if someone declared that it was red and round, that would merely reflect a very small aspect of it, and it's still possible that its backside might be rotten, blue and swollen, or that it might have a jagged cross-section. We should be able to regard the inclusivity of this thing called apple, from every perspective and from many different angles. That is to say, it is important to grant objects a more three-dimensional observation. Perhaps the way poetry finds expression is by taking materials that had once been reflected into reality and returning them to the realm of thought.

Until now I had been obsessed with the intersection of diagonals on a single plane. I had often failed to notice the lines passing over the space paralleling these diagonals, or the perpendicular lines dropping down into these diagonals. I wonder how much of the space is occupied not by black or white, but by a hazy vagueness that is neither black nor white. And what a joy it would be to open up the windows of a room with such mesh-like complexity. I feel the need to pry it open for myself.

At the exhibit I saw many completed paintings. Yes they might be quite accomplished, but these kinds of paintings are just not interesting. They represent a kind of completion within a single territory, or the halting of a movement—they are none other than the communication of an impasse. I was actually more attracted to the works that failed. That tumult seems indicative of potential. I also felt that there were many works that were influenced by film. For example, the distinction between silhouettes, and the light and darkness of black and white. There were van Goghs, and paintings with two suns, too.

I was so tired I could no longer feel my feet on the ground, but when I stepped outside, the brilliant young green stung my eyes.

MY NIGHTTIME

I've fallen into the habit of staying up late again. I sneak my brother's cigarette case out of the room next door, and when I smoke his Golden Bats I feel awake, not at all sleepy. It's not that they taste good or anything, but I've come to take pleasure in letting my thoughts wander as I smoke. I wonder how I've come to like the nighttime so much. The air feels clammy and seems to bear down upon the doors and window frames. The things that sparkled during the day disappear completely, and I begin to hear something pounding the earth. Perhaps it is the sound of the conversations and footsteps of the many people walking the streets, left over from the day along with a slight dampness. At some point the day got extinguished—that's all there is to it, but what a big difference it makes. A silent repose continues, as if everything has died. All things melt into the darkness of night, and stitches of time pass by close to my ears. If I sit very still there, I grow light as if I have shed my clothes—all my efforts, theories, resistances, and pretensions give way and I should become a good, honest person. I can tolerate anybody cracking the whip on me. If I am told to cry, I can wail like no other. I pull out these dusty little stones I've collected over a long period of time, and play with them. There are pumice stones from the Izu islands that give off a white powder, as well as obsidian, agate fragments, fossils with leaf veins, and sharp arrowheads that were used long ago by the Ainu people for bear hunting—all piled up in this little box. When I rub them with my sleeve, they give off a strange, clear light. It seems as if there is a mystical night coagulated inside each stone.

And then I think about the colors of leaves, the darkness of oceans, and of people sleeping. I realize that the most frightful things of this world as well as the most heinous things of the world take place within this vast darkness. On the other side of night, these things are already happening. And I alone keep watch over them.

KINUMAKI-SAN AND HIS POETRY COLLECTION, *PEDAL ORGAN*

Kinumaki-san, he blinks a lot when he speaks. That's when I start preparing myself for what he is about to say. And then he'll say something very funny in a not-so-funny way, which is really very funny. Once I learned the foxtrot while spinning a record with my finger because the springs on the gramophone were broken. Everyone from back then must have forgotten how we danced on the tatami mats, peeling back the carpeting. These old memories return to me, upon receiving *Pedal Organ* by Kinumaki-san. Such old-school musical accompaniment. I haven't seen you in a while—I wonder if you are well. Kinumaki-san is quite the dandy; he dangles an expensive tie around his neck as if it were nothing. He carries his walking stick like it bores him, and that somehow becomes him too. For Kinumaki-san, his tie and his hat may just as well be part of his body, like his hands and feet. It's as if his poetry, too, carries the body odor of its owner, just like his gloves and handkerchiefs.

Some of the poems in *Pedal Organ* are quite unruly, I must say. In them I hear meaningless, nonsensical music as if a fine lady just plunked herself down on the keys of a piano. Although I am mistrustful, I am attracted nonetheless to this carefree mode. I am in the habit of taking at face value anything I see with my eyes, so I am puzzled by the sight of the many muses leaping out of the bellows, as they are played by skillful feet. It is delightful that poetry can have so much fun while wearing normal clothes.

But I wonder if Kinumaki-san is really a cunning one. He never hits you from the front, but hides his sentiments further and further back, peeking through and smirking from between those five fingers.

My favorite poem from *Pedal Organ* is called "Apple Orchard Chronicle."

ON *BUCOLIC COMEDIES* BY EDITH SITWELL

Reading the Bon Shoten edition of the poetry collection *Bucolic Comedies* by Edith Sitwell, I am strangely reminded of a portrait of her I once saw. Her folded hands sporting a large ring, her wide triangular forehead, and dark, swaying shadow that appears to be lit by candlelight. Just like her outward appearance that creates an uncomfortable, sweaty feeling—like if you were not careful you might get washed away into some unknown depth—likewise I feel from these seventeen poems in *Bucolic Comedies* by this female British poet not a sentimental sweetness, but instead a kind of intense voluminousness. And then again, though it lacks the transparency of a van Gogh painted on a sheet of glass, it is nonetheless possible to hear in it a duet between the brightness of nature borne from the sun, and the undulations of the human heart. The beauty in Sitwell's poems are not forgeries gold-plated in moonlight, but rather an authentic kind of beauty that is tenacious like steel.

In a poem called "Père Amelot," she writes that the moon is "Like an Augustan coin." The image of jangling coins being fished up to the tops of poplars on a windy night is interesting. Compared to most other pastoral lyrics, it might seem that in her world of poetry the comb of a rooster, the gooseberry thorns, and the little stars are all merely actors in the theater of nature, but in fact, these objects of nature, filtered of reality, form beautiful silhouettes.

I think that "Nocturne" excerpted from *The Wooden Pegasus* is a strong poem.

In terms of learning more about postwar British poetry, the publication of this collection by this female poet, translated by Kitamura Tsuneo, is a truly wonderful event.

BOUQUET OF FOG

Today was a cold day. The sky was on the brink of snowing. Your lovely poetry collection, *Flowers of Fog*, landed in my hands, still wet from doing the laundry. As I warm my frozen fingers, each of your poems radiates its heat towards me.

What a pure and beautiful poetry collection, bursting with honesty and sparkling with rich emotion. I imagine a single young shoot growing straight up out of the snow—it is fitting for you who birthed this refined *esprit* and wisdom that flickers from the May sky in the Hokuriku region, bursting with multitudes of violet flowers upon withered branches. And I think about how the fruits of your heart, immune from any distortion, cast such blissful shadows across the earth. I am not familiar with the sound of the ocean nor with the color of the sky that always provide your musical accompaniment, but it has been a long time since I have recalled the breath-stopping days of snowstorm in my native Northern lands, or the streets lit by the white-light of the snow. With the cold air covering your heart like feathers, I wonder what kinds of shadows the Alps make in your eyes, or what kinds of sharp lights bring you to a shiver. Your poems have such naïve lines and vivid colors that are impossible to consider apart from this context.

I long to visit you in person. And to converse about some of my favorite memories—of horse-drawn sleigh bells, rubber boots, the snow piling up on rooftops, and those days when the mountains appear so close. This would allow me to also enjoy inhabiting the very landscape that raised you.

We own certain things—such as moments that are not to be lost. The poetry collection *Flowers of Fog* is, for us as well as for you, a beautiful memorial tree. I believe you will go over and beyond it. I believe that henceforth, too, you will create invisible, large shapes that are full of the girl-like curiosity and passion that is in *Flowers of Fog*.

Outside the winter is very cold, but I feel the warmth in people's hearts. Is it snowing in Takaoka. I send you my sincerest wishes for a grand publication event for *Flowers of Fog*, surrounded by female poets.

LIKE FAIRY TALES

From an early age I dreamed a lot of dreams. As soon as I woke up, I would carefully count them and set them aside while I washed my face and combed my hair, so that I could try to hold on to these illusions. Around then the stories I told were all things I had dreamt, and my friends would laugh and say, you're talking about your dreams again. I remember walking to school while describing a new dream about seeing a snowy road without a single footstep on it. It seems I had quite a lot of dreams every night.

What in reality was my very dull sense of seeing and hearing turned quite vivid in my dreams—something else altogether—playing tricks and working in various ways. It's strange how the colors were always so vivid. Some dreams were in sepia like old photographs, while in some dreams the ocean was green. Sometimes as I closed my eyes at night I would wish for things—to continue the previous night's dream, to hear that music one more time, or to go to Europe. In those childhood years when dreams are so important, my actual lived life was so full of loss, and little things to be sad about. That must be why, just as most people were going to sleep, my heart would awaken and make up dreams—I must have wanted to love and play like this, in the most natural way. And I alone lived, laughed, and fantasized within that dream space, trying to prevent myself from taking even a single step out.

I made my way through the daytime in a haze, but when evening came, these wonderfully detailed spirits flooded my empty head and filled up all the spaces. In my dreams, the dead never aged, broken objects had shapes, and there were no gaps in either time or space. It is a delightful thing to have everything moving forward in the present.

Come morning, it would feel like there were too many things that I should not let escape.

Nowadays I do not dream much. Even when I do, they are forgotten quickly. It is not because I am tired, but because there are no longer any friends to report my dreams to, and not only that, but my reality has all turned to dreams now, too.

WHEN PASSING BETWEEN TREES

Wearing glasses was not for the purpose of seeing things more clearly. That is to say, if what I see is limited by the width of my face, I might misperceive only that which appears before me, the sparks of the phenomenon itself often distracting me before I learn just how the thing spreads out or permeates. To see is not the same as knowing the result; it is for the purpose of reaching the end of one part of the phenomenon. Such are my thoughts as I walk through the wheat field. The wheat grows vigorously like a victor, shining in white rows against the black earth. I wonder if the sun in May isn't a little too bright for the Japanese poets of today. They speak only of dreams and illusions, failing to harmonize with this all-too-French air. What relationship could there be between their imagery and the row of trees on the other side? The negligence of having imported only the world of Leica into poetry only makes us a little dizzy—neither their pastry-like sweetness nor their enumerated language could be seen as having the freshness of the young leaves on the zelkova trees by the side of the path I walk. They lose themselves only when imitating others, and when that figure has been chipped away at, are quite tired. There is a clear beauty in the hazy scenery when I have removed my glasses, and there is also a hazy goodness in what I see clearly when my glasses are on. But to think that everyone must gaze into a single mirror and distinguish black from white is foolish. It is not so much about searching for boundaries, but rather the precise snapping together of the infinite allusions on either side of that single line, with the cross-sections of a leaping field of vision. And yet, the highs and lows of artistic rhythm are determined by whether that field of vision is near or far. I believe poetry is the study of language. Unlike spoken language, it is a language of the heart, not visible from the

surface. It is the filling of the air with words selected out of deep
contemplation. Not a gathering of the meanings of words spoken to
be spoken, but an attempt to say something, or to reflect something.
Very sparse and most strict, it is a skillfulness right on the brink of
burning out like a flame. It can mean to say one real thing within a
long conversation, or to go chasing after something from behind.

I step on a still-lit cigarette butt. Someone has already
gone ahead of me. His failure, and her error, lay in the finding of
something man-made in the discontinuities of this endless nature.
As I walk into the woods, I become aware of the roaring wind. I find
it hard to believe that Kashiwagi Shunzō, many of whose poems
were just like the sound of the wind, was in love with treetops—as
well as inorganic substances like the air and the wind. Rather, I
imagine it was quite the opposite. He must have written those use-
less things out of a desire to depict people at the moment the wind
passes through their bodies, or the sight of himself staring at whin-
nying ponies in the woods. Am I the only one who feels something
akin to suffering in the poetry of this man who wanted to portray
the human, stripped bare, but simply could not depict a person
shouting this, and so instead wrote only echoes, only the tracks left
behind by earlier passages? This intensity is better felt in his poem
called "Lightning" in the April issue of *Shii no ki*, rather than the
one called "Early Spring," published in the May issue. Master of
the language of trees and quite enraged, he emerges before us by
breaking through the scenery. On the other hand, "Life in the
Countryside" by Ema Shōko, provides the usual inexplicable plea-
sure that is like listening to music that is out of focus. No matter
what the situation, she never tries to put things in focus. We feel a
bit lost. And then just at that moment, a vividly beautiful curve. I
always expect great things from Hirano Jinkei, and he has never
disappointed. "Divergence" is a deftly constructed poem. In "A mo-
ment with an old friend," Uchida Tadashi depicts the fragility of
emotions that are toppled like dominos before kind words. No real
object is visible, but its projection casts blurry rings at our chests.
Such are the things I feel from the poems of Uchiyama Yoshirō. In

both "Daily life" and "Contemplation" from the March issue, he seems to express an interior symmetry using only straight lines. "Roof mechanic" by Abe Tamotsu is a sweet lyric poem. We always imagine the picture of a young girl with a bouquet of flowers, wonder if it isn't a bit too distant in terms of music—and the thorns of those roses are shining like clear crystal needles. "Song of March" by Takamatsu Akira seems rather gentle. But the seasonal winds are no longer pastorals. Like those footsteps, they slap us on the cheek as they pass by. Walking through the woods, I discover a single tree with very smooth bark. It is unfamiliar to me, and so I wonder what it is. I read Odakane Jirō's work for the first time. "Song of Stone" is like looking at the jagged breaks in refracted light. Something akin to viscosity indicates a faint brightness.

The trees stand silent. As if to conquer time, for the sake of a thousand years. Purity was not the difference between water and beer. I found being unable to see the sky from between the trees suffocating.

EMA SHŌKO AND MY RADIANT DREAMS

Ema-san is a cheerful and energetic lady who always seems to be having a good time. All the more so when we meet up in Ginza—the reds and yellows of her clothes reflect the brilliant colors of the city in the background, making Ema-san all the more beautiful. Walking with her, I often catch her singing lightly or keeping time with her fingers. It appears as if she enjoys a special music being played somewhere, that she alone can distinguish out of the cacophony of the city—I believe that she alone gets it, and that I do not. She seems to stroll around Ginza quite a bit. I feel more comfortable in my dark village at night, with the toads croaking and the owls hooting, whereas Ema-san in Ginza is like this: *Oh I often see Jō-san from* Bungeihanronsha, *I saw Kitasono-san walking around without a hat, I saw Gyō-san, he was so tan he looked black, probably because he plays tennis, I saw Komatsu Kiyoshi-san twice in one day, and then we had tea at Columbin, and Komatsu-san said, "Ema-san you must have gotten married," and when I asked why, he said "because you've lost weight," and that irritated me so I told him that I would indeed report to him when I got married, I think he must have been drunk, that Komatsu-san—* and as she goes on like that, this season in Ginza opens up wide like a parasol———I'm imagining these streets where you can get a pot of flowers for a ten-sen coin; or stores with tanks of tropical fish; or the lively ways of acquaintances who I greet with a smile even though I haven't made the effort to see them in a while—and it all makes me want to run away from this dark village that seems to harbor ghosts, get rustled by the rumbling train and then spit out right in the middle of Ginza. The Ginza that Ema-san speaks of is a beautiful, musical city with a fast beat, in strange contrast to the hot and shadeless Ginza that I sometimes find myself trudging through.

Ema-san's healthy, boundless energy is contagious—so I, too, feel more energetic, and I hear my voice jump up an octave. I can hear it rising, getting too high, and yet I can't stop myself. Ema-san has many attractive words in her possession. Or rather, perhaps she just has that particular effect, even when she talks about boring things. And it seems that it all tends to come out when she's talking to me. Ema-san can't hold anything back; she talks like she's trying to prevent it all from overflowing completely. Usually they are very happy thoughts, and there are times that I am so blinded by them that my words get caught and I am unable to respond. There are so many great things about her, and she's able to express them to the outside world with ease and honesty. She is beautiful like some kind of luminous body, illuminating those who are near her with that light. *That's it, that's all there is to it,* she'll say, and I'll give her a look that says *I know there's more, there's more you're going to say.* I can't remember where I first met Ema-san, or when we became close friends. She may have just started acting like we were close, when I wasn't paying attention, or maybe it's because when she laughs, I laugh, as if a spell has been cast on me, and that when she is acting lighthearted I find myself copying that, and before I know it, there is something that wasn't in me before that has steadily made its way inside.

I'm rotting! Cheer me up! On the other end of the phone line she sounds a bit troubled, so I go over expecting to cheer her up, but then when I see her I have a big laugh because she's bemoaning the most trifling little thing. I'm usually the one who needs cheering up, and I must seem like I really need it, because she says *Cheer up, what do you want to eat?* Perhaps people get hungry when things aren't going well. And I say that I want to eat the most delicious thing in the world, and then she takes me out to eat until I get sleepy.

We only see each other once a month or so. When we meet, the conversation picks up as if we left off only the day before. We've hardly ever talked about poetry or literature or anything. If I bring up something to do with poetry, Ema-san looks kind of squeamish, maybe she is kind of embarrassed about it. I don't even know what kinds of books she reads. I've seen some theater history books on her shelf, from back when she had joined the Tsukiji-za and was seriously trying to get into theater. Every time I see her work published I wonder when she wrote it, or what her face looks like when she is writing a poem, silly things like that. Ema-san loves the ocean. I remember we were once at Ōmori-Kaigan, resting our chins on the concrete wall staring into the darkening ocean and talking about going abroad. Right where the Tokyo Bay Steamship turned on its light to enter the bay. That summer, there was that little trip we took to the Izu islands with those magazine editors. It was very choppy and the whole ship was getting swallowed by the waves, and the men and children and everyone was completely seasick—but Ema-san alone was perfectly fine. We were jealous and called her "female pirate." This female pirate told us that if only we had gotten shipwrecked, we might have washed up all the way in San Francisco. This reckless female pirate claims she wishes she could have been washed away indeed. The Ōmori ocean was murky and full of driftwood. We joked about how you could ride a freight ship to Marseilles for only 300 yen, or that there were jobs in Chile for Japanese school teachers. And Ema-san would say, *Oh I want to go, I really want to go,* and it really seemed like she might just up and go. Other times, we would talk about opening a trendy shop in Ginza together, maybe a bookstore, maybe a cake shop, and we'd daydream about the fun we'd have spending the money we made. And so our dreams matched up very nicely. Ema-san had a sparkle in her eye. And then a thought would occur to me. Even if we harbored similar dreams, it was Ema-san that somehow had the ability to realize them and be satisfied. Me, I'm just a dreamer. But I do believe that Ema-san has the ability and opportunities to realize these dreams. Ema-san never gets tired, and she's very much at peace with her own happiness. But at home she's a bit spoiled. She's fawned over like a butterfly or flower. The other day Ema-san said she just doesn't like women like Anna Karenina. And then we got to talking about wives in novels, and how some wives are just so greedy. Fortunately neither of us are married yet, so we felt free to badmouth wives. Ema-san said she's been attracted to older men lately. I don't know much about her past, so I don't know, but I wonder if this was some kind of change of heart(?)

DIARY

October 16th

Early morning, I open the window and see a hearse exiting the hospital gates. When I see the black shape making its way through the smoky rain, I feel my heart stop. I regret having looked outside. When Dr. Aoki makes his rounds in the afternoon he says I don't need to have the surgery. I had been hoping for the operation to slice into that space under my chest and hack away at all the bad parts, annihilate that bug of a disease that has been tormenting me—but now I am filled with regret and uncertainty. I feel sick all day from the image of that black shape in the morning.

21st

In the morning I don't feel so well, and doze off a little. I feel more energetic in the evening, though my fever has gone up. I have them cut me some canned pineapple. I feel all the better after they wash my hands and feet. Yuri-san comes by. She says she is going to Otsuka to buy socks, and that she is going to buy some nougat and eat it on the way home. Right after that, my brother comes. He seems really busy. He pulls out the mail from his bag. He tells me what's going on outside of this vacation home, staying until well past nine. I'm glad when it feels like my night has been significantly shortened. He gives me a dose of sleeping pills. I read journals until around midnight. And then I take the pills and go to sleep. At around one o'clock I suddenly feel quite ill, and ask for a shot.

October 22nd Sunny

Maybe it's the shot from the night before, but I feel very drowsy.
The morning sun pours in through the window. I sunbathe on my
bed. Bathing my whole body in the autumn sun and drenched in
sweat, I feel very good. I've been in the hospital for two weeks now.
The people in the hallway are bustling around because Dr. Inada
is making his rounds today. They give me clean white sheets. A
cluster of dragonflies flies higher and higher into the blue sky, then
disappears. I wonder where they come from, so many of them.
When I look out the window and see students and workers passing
by on the street, moving their healthy-looking limbs, I, too, long for
thicker legs and hands. I stick my arms up in the air and rotate them
two or three times, but they look skinny and dark and dirty to me
and it brings me down. I tell Dr. Aoki that I don't like being in the
hospital because I can't sleep at night, and he says that I should go
home then. Today they are supposed to be determining the name
of my illness. Yuri-san comes in the evening. She talks about school,
then goes home. My brother does not come.

October 23rd

Every morning I wake up in a strangely drowsy state, the effects of
the painkillers not completely worn off. I'm happy to have a decent
morning, like I've been having recently. Today I have an appetite,
and feel like eating anything. I receive the X-ray treatment. For
thirty minutes. By dinner time I feel sick and can't eat. I wonder if
it was because of the X-ray. After dinner, I lay sleeping with a wet
towel on my chest, and Yuri-san and my brother come in. Yuri-
san shows me enlargements of photos from her trip to Hakone,
and pictures from school. We look at the albums together, with
Nozawa-san and everybody. I receive a gift from Hideo-san, from
Nikko. I ask my brother for *senmaizuke*, pickled red beets. At noon,
the calligraphy teacher, Ms. Aoyama's sister, brings beautiful
pomegranates. My mother is delighted, saying she has never seen a

pomegranate before. At eleven o'clock I get a shot of morphine and fall into a deep sleep. Of special note: for the first time in two weeks I was able to walk down the stairs to get to the X-ray room.

24th

A succession of ill-feeling, monotonous days where I can't even remember how the day passed by. Laying in bed staring at the sky, the things to come and the things that have passed all blend into one, and I do not like it. One of the clouds looks like Mussolini's face, and that was funny. It seems that the X-ray wears me down quite a bit. My brother came after the lights were turned out, sat on the edge of my bed, and we talked quietly after people had gone to sleep. I told him how I longed for good pickles, and also asked for the books I wanted to read. Today I read about half of an essay collection by Hyakken. I chose not to have the shot, and to put up with my pain. I'm working on training my will, so I no longer care how effective these drugs are.

25th

A day when I don't feel like saying anything. The doctor wakes me from my morning nap. As I go down the hallway and the stairs to get to the X-ray room, the nurses bustling about energetically at work seem strangely dazzling to me. Watching the cars go down the street makes me want to break into a run. In Hyakken's essays, he wrote about Sōseki's death. Apparently in the autopsy they found that his stomach was torn and pools of blood had accumulated in his intestines. I couldn't hold back the tears. In the evening Yuri-san comes. She tells me that her grandmother from Aoyama had passed away. And that the puppy still hasn't opened its eyes. I see her out to the front door.

26th

My brother comes early in the afternoon. After a while, Obasan from Nakano, Nēsan, and Kei come to visit. They give me a basket of fruit. Kei tells me he has learned three words in English. Dog, Cat, Peanuts. Today I feel quite good, which makes me happy. Kei sits on the bed and shows me how he can draw dolls and streamlined shapes. In the evening, Kobayashi Tsuneko-san comes by. From around the time she leaves, the rain picks up. During his evening rounds, Dr. Aoki smiles and asks if I can hang in there. I am thinking of trying to make it through without a shot. I might be okay because I didn't nap during the day. Around eight o'clock, Ono-san comes with Yuri-san. In the middle of the night, there is a big fight outside and it wakes me up. I receive a letter from Ritsuko-san.

27th Wind and rain

A violent storm, with thunder and lightning. I see the large trees swaying outside my window. Perhaps because of the weather, I am not feeling very good—I don't even want to speak. My brother comes in spite of the pouring rain. I had assumed that no one would come today, so that makes me very happy. My stomach does not feel right.

29th

In the morning, Nēsan brings Kei. They bring me roses and a toy cat. Kei again draws funny pictures at my bedside and then goes home. They take an X-ray. I don't feel as tired as usual. Dr. Inada comes around late in the evening. I couldn't hear my brother clearing his throat. They apply a compress all through the night. I am able to go without a shot. I am ever so grateful for my mother, who takes care of me without even loosening her *obi* sash.

30th
It's a nice day. Just that simple fact makes me tear up in one eye.
There is nothing as painful as trying to eat breakfast. In the afternoon
the pain in my stomach eases up. My brother had come while I was
asleep. He cheers me up in various ways, with stories about our
aunt in Yoichi who had sent apples. People are putting aside their
work to attend to me, and yet I feel like my illness is not my own. I
just don't feel like I own it. I want to get better quickly. I want to eat
dinner together at the small table in our house in Setagaya.

31st
I am in pain all day and receive three shots. Nēsan comes. She will
be stopping by the Hosaka home. They take an X-ray. It was a rough
day. The sun is so bright I can't stand it.

November 1st
My brother had said he was going to Yugawara, so today is a quiet
day with no visitors. I can see all the students walking along the
other side of the street. It's a holiday, the weather is nice, not the
kind of day to be indoors. I read Kielland's short stories. They're
pretty good. At night, a shot of *papiato* painkiller.

November 2nd
Momota-san's wife comes, along with Nēsan. I receive a carnation.
Its subtle scent fills the room. Hosaka-san's wife, Saburō, and Yasuo
come to visit. I have a bit of a fever, my back hurts and I cannot
stand up. I eat apples and pears. In the afternoon I chat in quite a
loud voice.

ACKNOWLEDGMENTS

Thank you: To Eugene, without whom so much of my work could not be accomplished. To my family, for ongoing love and support. To my kids, for their patience with their hardworking mom. To Eric Selland, Matt Treyvaud, Hitomi Yoshio, for extremely valuable insights. Thanks also to Jeffrey Angles, Toshiko Ellis, Ono Yū, Patrick Durgin, and Miwako Ozawa. And to the editors at Canarium: Joshua Edwards, Robyn Schiff, Nick Twemlow, and Lynn Xu.

This translation is based on the beautifully edited and produced Sagawa Chika *Zenshishū, Shinpan* (*Collected Works of Sagawa Chika*, new edition), edited and published by Ono Yū (Shinkaisha, 2010). Many thanks to Ono-san for years of work on Chika's poetry, which includes the publication of a book of English-Japanese translations by Chika Sagawa, who continues to uncover additional poems that Chika had written.

I wish to give my deepest thanks to Mika Kasuga, for her steadfast support and without whom this new edition would not exist. Thanks to Chris Clemans. To Allison Levy and Dashiell Wasserman for helping me move the work on Sagawa forward in new and exciting ways.

Many thanks, always, to John Granger. Additional thanks to the people who have written reviews, taught classes, led reading groups, translated poems, judged prizes, as well as occasioned panels, readings, events, and other art inspired by Chika's poetry—including but not limited to: Adrienne Raphel, Alba Doval Rodriguez, Alys Moody, Andrew Badr, Andrew Campana, Aron Aji, Brian Evenson, Corey Wakeling, Don Mee Choi, Eileen Myles, Emily Wolahan, Eric Ekstrand, Forrest Gander, Hannah Ensor, Jane Wong, Jen Hofer, Jen Scappettone, Joel Katelnikoff, Katrina Dodson, Kazuno Fujii, Keith Vincent, Kendall Heitzman, Kyongmi Park, Laura Sims,

Lindsay Webb, Lisa Samuels, Mariko Nagai, Michael Holtmann, Midori Endoh, Noriko Mizuta, Samuel Perry, Taylor Mignon, Vivek Narayanan, Zachary Schomburg, and Zack Newick.

This translation has also been supported by the following fellowships, institutions, and programs: NEA Literary Translation Grant, Witter Bynner Poetry Translator Residency at the Santa Fe Art Institute, Japan-US Friendship Commission's Creative Artists Program, and the Japan Foundation's Support Program for Translation and Publication on Japan.

Grateful acknowledgment goes to the editors of the following journals and publications, for publishing earlier versions of some of these translations: *Asymptote, Aufgabe, Bat City Review, Calque, Columbia Poetry Review, D Press, Factorial, Fascicle, HOW2*, PEN American Center website, *Poetry, Thuggery & Grace, Two Lines, Two Lines Online*, and *Verse*. Excerpts of the work have also been published in *The Other Voices International Project: A Cyber-anthology* edited by Roger Humes, *Ekota Bungaku* Issue 63 (Sagawa Chika feature in Japan), *Currently & Emotion: Translations* edited by Sophie Collins (Test Centre, 2016), and *Global Modernists on Modernism—An Anthology* edited by Alys Moody and Stephen J. Ross (Bloomsbury Academic, 2020). The following books have also featured Sagawa's work: *To the Vast Blooming Sky by Chika Sagawa* (Seeing Eye Books chapbook, Los Angeles, California, 2006) and *Mouth: Eats Color—Sagawa Chika Translations, Anti-Translations, and Originals* by Sawako Nakayasu and Chika Sagawa (Rogue Factorial, 2011). "Day of Snow" was selected by Emily Hunt to be featured in the Los Angeles Poetry in Motion program and was displayed on LA Metro buses in April 2018. An excerpt from "Shapes of Clouds" was engraved in a paver stone as part of the site-specific art installation, *Dawn Chorus* by Brent Wahl and Laynie Browne, a Public Art Commission by the City of Philadelphia's Percent for Art Program (2018). The poem "Backside" was a source of inspiration for *Night Eats Color* (2019), a composition by Robert Gibson for an instrumental chamber ensemble of ten players, World Premiere performance by Inscape Chamber Orchestra, Richard Scerbo, conductor, April 7, 2019.

ABOUT THE AUTHOR

SAGAWA CHIKA (real name Kawasaki Chika) was born in 1911 in Hokkaido, Japan. In 1928 she moved to Tokyo and quickly integrated into the literary avant-garde community. She published her work frequently in the influential journal *Shi to Shiron* (Poetry and Poetics), and is considered by many to be the first female Modernist poet. Stomach cancer took her life at the age of twenty-four, at which point her poems were collected and edited by Ito Sei and published as *Sagawa Chika Shishū* (Collected Poems of Sagawa Chika, Shōrinsha, 1936). Later, a more complete collected works, including her prose, in memoriam writings from poets, and a complete bibliography, was published as *Sagawa Chika Zenshishū* (Collected Works of Sagawa Chika) by Shinkaisha in 1983. In 2010, her *Collected Poems* was republished by Shinkaisha, which also in 2011 published a new book collecting Sagawa's translations from English-language poetry, including poems by Charles Reznikoff, James Joyce, and Mina Loy.

ABOUT THE TYPE

The principal text of this Modern Library edition was set in a digitized version of Janson, a typeface that dates from about 1690 and was cut by Nicholas Kis (1650–1702), a Hungarian working in Amsterdam. The original matrices have survived and are held by the Stempel foundry in Germany. Hermann Zapf (1918–2015) redesigned some of the weights and sizes for Stempel, basing his revisions on the original design.